T0354574

Commanding the Forces

the

Forces

The Ministry of Intercession

GENEVA M. HUNTER

WESTBOW
PRESS®
A DIVISION OF THOMAS NELSON
& ZONDERVAN

All Scripture quotations, unless otherwise indicated,
are taken from the King James Version

Scripture quotations taken from the Amplified® Bible (AMP),
Copyright © 2015 by The Lockman Foundation
Used by permission. www.Lockman.org

WestBow Press books may be ordered through booksellers or by contacting:

WestBow Press
A Division of Thomas Nelson & Zondervan
1663 Liberty Drive
Bloomington, IN 47403
www.westbowpress.com
1 (866) 928-1240

ISBN: 978-1-5127-6401-7 (sc)
ISBN: 978-1-5127-6402-4 (hc)
ISBN: 978-1-5127-6400-0 (e)

Library of Congress Control Number: 2016918908

Print information available on the last page.

WestBow Press rev. date: 11/08/2016

Contents

Dedication

This book is dedicated to my loved ones:

My son, Byron C. McDade, whose now in heaven with Jesus. His unwavering faith and trust in God was a true inspiration to me, and will always be a reminder to me of how real unfeigned faith looks in and on a saint of God. I'm forever thankful to God for knowing you, son.

And to my mother, Bertha McDade, whose also now in heaven with Jesus. She taught me how to pray. I often think of the first time as a little girl seeing mama kneeling beside the bed praying to God for all her children and her family. I also remember kneeling beside her as she taught me the Lord's prayer.

And to my husband, Ed, for your patience and encouragement over the years.

And to my very wise and precious grandson Jeffery (Yank).

And to my dad, Allen, who is still just as strong as ever, both spiritually and physically at age 96.

And to my prayer partner, Tammy, and to my cousin, Dorothy. Thank you, both, for always being faithful, mighty prayer warriors and mighty women of God.

Preface

Commanding the Forces is written as a call to arms for all of God's intercessors *practicing and non-practicing; saved and unsaved.* Many of you have already begun to realize that there is something happening to you, a stirring in your souls, if you will. You are, most likely, experiencing a strong desire to go higher in the things of God. In addition, you have a deep yearning and desire for more, but you are not sure how to pursue it. Neither are you yet convinced that you are being summoned by God nor are you sure whether or not you really want it to be God. There are a vast number of intercessors in the same predicament who are not convinced whether or not he or she is ready to step aside long enough to inquire deeper. *Commanding the Forces* is written to open the blinded eyes of some and to facilitate a quest in the hearts of others who desire to be pleasing to God. As a result, some will start to become aware of who they are, why they are, and where they are destined to go. If you will allow Him, God will use *Commanding the Forces* to help you understand what has really been going on in your life. He will reveal to you why you have been under such severe attacks from the enemy all of your days. He will also reveal to you why there are certain things you cannot do or be a participant of. Finally, He will reveal to you why you have always been different.

Now is the time for the power and authority God has placed in you to be unleashed in the earth for the purposes which He intended from the foundation of the world. As a called intercessor, you have been called to take charge and defeat the enemy. You have been called to tear down the strongholds. You have been called to stand in the gap for God's people. God's intercessors are now being summoned out of the unknown in order to walk in his or her destinies to defeat the plans of the enemy. Unfortunately, some of the ones who have been called are not necessarily in the church, just yet. Because the enemy has been bombarding them with such vicious attacks, they're not even sure what they believe, at this point. The enemy is doing this in order to try and prevent he or she from coming into the kingdom and fulfilling their call. Because a praying saint is very frightful to the enemy, he will do everything he's allowed to try and keep you confused about who you really are. God will use *Commanding the Forces* to awaken the body of Christ out of their slumber, remove the scales from the eyes of some, and educate others concerning the very powerful and often misunderstood ministry of intercession.

Acknowledgement

All Praise, Glory, and Honor to God for using me as a tool to write *Commanding the Forces* for such a time as this. The ultimate purpose of this project is to bring God glory, edify the body of Christ, educate others who are trying to determine what is happening in their lives, and expose the true intent of the enemy as well as how to take our rightful authority in the earth as the body of Christ. I thank my husband for his love and assistance in caring for my 96-year old dad so I could spend the necessary time hearing God and putting into writing what I believe He has been speaking into my spirit. I am also thankful to my prayer partners, church family, and pastors for being a true inspiration. I am so very thankful for and to Westbow Press and its very capable and inspirational staff for the opportunity to present this work to the body of Christ and beyond.

Introduction

We are now witnessing the greatest onslaught of demonic attacks that have ever been unleashed upon the earth. *Commanding the Forces* is designed to arm God's intercessors and the body of Christ to be ready for and participate in the greatest end-time harvest this world has ever witnessed. *Commanding the Forces* will serve as a reminder to the bulk of the body of Christ what we possess as called intercessors, as a wake-up call to those of us who have been lulled to sleep, and remove the scales from the eyes of those who are currently outside of the Body due to the fact that they have been blinded by the enemy. First and foremost, it is explicitly written to the church to inform us of why we are witnessing the hostile takeover of the world by demonic forces at breakneck speed. *Commanding the Forces* will also serve to identify our God-given weapons and show us how to use these weapons that our Lord and Savior Jesus Christ have endowed us with for such a time as this. Furthermore, it will serve to educate the saints of God concerning the evil tactics of the enemy, answer some pertinent questions by using scripture, as well as expose the enemy to the ones who are seeking as why he or she are experiencing such unprecedented strong attacks upon their lives. These vicious attacks are being unleashed upon both the saved and unsaved. *Commanding the Forces* will allow God to input some things into our spirits as well as take some things out in order to prepare us as His elite force to be released into a world that is in dire need of spiritual help. *Commanding the Forces* will not only serve as an addition to our Christian arsenal but as a life-altering, invaluable tool to not only enable us to become but remain victorious in fulfilling our call to occupy until He comes. In lieu of these catastrophic and brutal attacks from the enemy, many are asking both God and the church some very valid questions. Some of the questions are, *if we have been commanded to do the same works as Jesus did, and if we are in Christ Jesus and if He is in us, and if we have been given all power and all authority over all the power of the enemy, why, then, are we witnessing such carnage in our nation and in our world?* If we stop and take a sincere and honest look at our priorities, the answer will be obvious. Clearly, there are some very important truths that we are missing and/or are not comprehending. Thereby, causing us to remain stagnant in our relationships with the Lord while continually being pulverized by the enemy. We are being destroyed because of what we do not know, and in most instances, we're failing to utilize the greatest weapon upon this earth—the Word-filled, Holy Ghost filled prayer. In addition to *Commanding the Forces* being a reminder to some and a revelation to others of this weapon that God has entrusted us to have in our possession, it will also serve as a handy accessible resource to keep us cognizant of who we are and what we're capable of doing in the world for the kingdom of God. By lacking the necessary understanding and knowledge for these times, we're failing to maximize and operate in what we have been given as we should. This has not only caused a significant number of the body of Christ to be consistently brutalized and even destroyed by the enemy of our souls, but it has also caused a delay in our reaching an unknown number of people who are desperately looking for the kingdom of God.

After reading *Commanding the Forces*, many questions will be answered as well as some eyes being opened to the fact that the body of Christ is now in receipt of all power and authority in Jesus' name. It will be a reminder to the saints of God concerning its mandate to operate in that authority. It will also serve as a catalyst to kick start the operation of all of the dormant gifts and weapons that are in our possession. We will also get Biblically based, detailed instruction as to how to correctly use these gifts and weapons that God have placed in our possession. Since, we are quickly running out of time to reach the souls we have been mandated to reach on our respective watches, attaining this super important understanding and knowledge is critical. We cannot begin to complete our assignments until we take that first step. Let's get started on what we were created to do in the earth for such a time as this! The scripture reads, "Therefore said He unto them, The harvest truly is great, but the laborers are few; pray ye therefore the Lord of the harvest, that He would send forth labourers into His harvest." Luke 10:2.

Chapter One

INTERCESSOR

And I sought for a man among them, that should make up the hedge, and stand in the gap before me for the land, that I should not destroy it; but I found none. Ezekiel 22:30

HAT AN UNBELIEVABLE state that the church finds itself in at this juncture in the earth! Instead of the enemy becoming alarmed when he hears the name *intercessor,* he instead shakes his evil head and continues on with his destructive behavior of wreaking havoc in the world. Unfortunately, this is happening in the body of Christ as well. Painfully, there are just as many falling prey to the enemy and becoming casualties inside of the church as there are outside of the church. A very large number of these casualties are or rather were called intercessors. There are an overwhelming number of so-called intercessors who have practically given up due to being ill prepared for the job. So many of us who are genuinely called just jumped in feet first without seeking God and following the correct procedure which has led to disastrous outcomes. As a result, we now have a lot of perplexed, gun-shy individuals who are beginning to doubt whether or not we were really called to the ministry of intercession. Consequently, the enemy has had

1

free reign to keep bombarding the church and the world with his evil agenda. *Commanding the Forces* will take us through the God definitions and God procedures for not only accepting our call as intercessors but also successfully fulfilling our call to bring the enemy down in Jesus's name.

After we're born again, every saint of God must be a serious student of the Bible. At the onset of our studies, we're taught to recognize that we are spiritual beings. Even though we inhabit physical bodies, we only live in them temporarily until we've fulfilled our destinies here on the earth. As we continue to be taught both by reading of the Word and by the indwelling of the Holy Spirit, we come to the knowledge that God is a God of order—and there is an order that has been set forth by God for humankind. This order is to be, especially, practiced and adhered to in the church and the body of Christ. In our study of the Word, we also come to the knowledge that each one of us has a particular place to inhabit and a particular path to follow that has been designed just for us, individually. This is a pre-ordained path that we alone can follow. There is a position I am created to occupy, and there is a position God has carved out just for you as well. As we learn more, we come to the realization that since we are born again, we should no longer walk after things in the flesh but after the things in the Spirit. God requires us to take up our assigned positions in the spiritual realm. As we begin to ascertain our calling as intercessors, we learn God has placed certain innate assets within us that allow us to successfully facilitate our particular assignments. He has called each of us to perform in a certain role for a distinct purpose that was designed just for us individually. An intercessor is called to rule in the spiritual realm of prayer. We are called to fight the enemy on our knees. Although this is indeed true, it is only a part of the calling of an intercessor. Unfortunately, the majority of us who are called intercessors are still trying to fulfill the prayer-mode part of our calling and have not yet progressed enough for God to move us on into the other areas of fulfilling our call as intercessors. As a result, there are a lot of frustrated and confused intercessors trying to ascertain what is going on. We are getting fatigued and are being offended in God because we are not getting the results we desire in our prayer lives. A large majority of us have each become akin to being a whipping boy instead of an intercessor. The enemy is taking advantage of the fact that we're entering into battles ill-equipped, and he is enjoying making a public display of us to the world. Because we lack the knowledge and are void of the full understanding of the call to intercessor, the enemy is truly stealing, killing, and destroying the body of Christ at the same rate as the world. In developing an understanding of how to war in the spirit, every one of us as saints should learn who the enemy is, learn how to fight our enemy, learn what kind of weapons to use in the fight, and learn how to use those weapons effectively and efficiently. Our foundation, the weapon of prayer, is the greatest weapon we have as saints of God. In doing battle with the enemy of our souls, we must not expect that a casual prayer life will suffice. In order to be successful in defeating the enemy, we must delve deeper into the realm of prayer. We must learn to intercede. In learning about the attributes of prayer, we must become familiar with the biblical definition for deep intercessory prayer. The Bible itself holds the key to this understanding, and it is designed by God to take us into a deeper, more intimate understanding of how to do battle in the spirit and win as did our Lord Jesus Christ. In order to get there, I believe we need to explore in more detail the definition of intercessory prayer, the church's role, the call to prayer, how to get our prayers answered, the lifestyle of a prayer warrior (intercessor), the authority that has been given to the saints, and how to walk in that authority. The terms *intercessor*, *intercession*, and *the ministry of intercession*, although related, are each unique in their definitions and attributes. These terms are sometimes used interchangeably within the Christian community without a thorough working knowledge of their individual definitions and attributes.

It is true that the textbook definition for *intercessor* is someone who petitions on behalf of another; intercessors are those who serve as the go-between for someone with God, or they stand in the gap for another individual. In addition to the textbook definition, I believe and I have experienced that God's definition of an intercessor is, first of all, we are someone who is saved and born again. We must be someone who has been delivered from the kingdom of darkness and is now completely entered into the kingdom of light. We must know who we are and to whom we belong. We need to be someone whose eyes have been opened and made aware of the need to pray for those who are saved and unsaved. We need to be someone who has been tested and tried—someone whom God can trust. In other words, all saints are qualified to intercede on behalf of another, but I do not believe that all saints are called, specifically, to the ministry of intercession. I take this stance because I believe that it has been made abundantly clear in the scripture, and God has shown us, in multiple areas, that there is some prayer that requires a dedication that goes beyond a casual prayer life. He cannot use us when we have the mindset that we might pray or we might not, which is dependent upon how we are feeling at the time. This kind of attitude will not suffice. God is looking for the willing and obedient. God said, "I sought for a man among them, that should make up the hedge, and stand in the gap before me for the land, that I should not destroy it; but I found none." In Ezekiel 22:30. I believe this scripture clearly teaches us that God was not just looking for anyone to pray but for someone that was different and unusual. God was looking for someone, in particular, to

4

intercede on behalf of an entire city so that He would not have to destroy it. Intercessory prayer takes us to a place that cannot be reached without God and the Holy Spirit taking us there. This is a place that is totally void of our own mind, will, and emotions. It is a place where the intercessor is able to download a message directly from Almighty God concerning for whom and for what to pray. These are sometime very sensitive and secret items. When I say secret, I mean they are even a secret to the recipients of the prayers. This is why it is of the utmost importance to be someone whom God can trust—someone who will not stop no matter how long it takes. As an example of this trustworthiness, I believe we see this is beautifully portrayed in the book of Luke, where it shows us two of the saints who I believe were called, specifically, to the ministry of intercession and explicitly trusted by God. I am referring to Simeon and the prophetess Anna. The scripture reads:

> And, behold, there was a man in Jerusalem, whose name was Simeon and the same man was just and devout, waiting for the consolation of Israel; and the Holy Ghost was upon him. And it was revealed unto him by the Holy Ghost, that he should not see death before he had seen the Lord's Christ … And there was one Anna, a prophetess the daughter of Phanuel, of the tribe of Aser; she was of a great age, and had lived with an husband seven years from her virginity; And she was a widow of about fourscore and four years, which departed not from the temple but served God with fastings and prayers night and day. (Luke 2:25–26, 36–37).

Both Simeon and Anna were Holy Ghost–filled prayer warriors who were looking for the coming of the Lord Jesus Christ. They both were sent to the temple by the Spirit of God at the same time, and they both blessed the Lord Jesus and gave praise to God. The Bible does not make us privy to the exact time and place that the two saints received the revelation from God as to the identity of Jesus. Likewise, we were not made aware of how and when God revealed to them the exact time Jesus would be brought to the temple in Jerusalem by His parents to be presented to the Lord. We do know through the scripture that Simeon and Anna were prayer warriors and intercessors who both heard from God to pray for the coming of the Lord Jesus Christ. Finally, we do know that these two intercessors were entrusted with some very sensitive and powerful information that would, literally, forever change the course of mankind.

The Bible also uses the term *watchman* for a person who is called to intercede on behalf of another. A watchman's job is to be awake and watching while others are asleep—often spiritually speaking. Our job is to warn both saved and unsaved individuals of any spiritual danger that we perceive by the Spirit of God to be headed in their direction. God takes the job of a watchman so seriously that He declares that if the watchman does not perform his or her duties in warning the sinner, then He will require the blood of that sinner at the watchman's hand. The scripture reads,

> "But if the watchman see the sword come and blow not the trumpet, and the people be not warned; if the sword come, and take any person from among them, he is taken away in his iniquity; but his blood will I require at the watchman's hand. So thou O son of man, I have set thee a watchman unto the house of Israel, therefore thou shalt hear

the word of my mouth, and warn them from me."
Ezekiel 33:6–7.

Intercessors are the ones that are called to go before others in prayer and spiritually cut through walls and/or tear down strongholds. This is accomplished in the spiritual realm so that others can begin to see and follow a path through to God. Intercessors are on the spiritual front lines, so to speak. We are called to be the soldiers/warriors that are called to protect, defend, and to cover in prayer and to do spiritual warfare on behalf of others. Intercessors are an elite force designated by God to stand in the gap for the body of Christ. The intercessor to the body of Christ is akin to what the Special Operations Forces are to the military. We are specifically organized, trained, and equipped to conduct and support special operations for the military of God. We are not necessarily known by everyone, but we are strategic and precise in our field. An intercessor is trained by God. In fact, our entire lives are training courses set up by God for our calling. Because we are trained by God, we are someone that frightens the enemy like no other. There are many reasons for this as we will discover as we proceed into a deeper more intimate search of the Word of God via *Commanding the Forces*.

Because our calling as intercessors require us to be one twenty-four hours a day, seven days a week, we have been given the capability to intercede in our sleep. When the Lord awakens us intercessors out of our deep sleep, we, as mature intercessors automatically awaken in a prayer and warfare mode as prompted by the Holy Spirit. We, the intercessor can be anywhere (at the grocery store, at home in our kitchens cooking a meal, or cleaning, etc.) and be able to intercede. God can speak to our hearts and lead us to pray for a particular person, situation, or place at any time and/or anywhere. Sometimes, we will just be prompted to pray in the Spirit. There are other times an intercessor will be called away to a place that has been designated by God to separate ourselves in order to listen and pray. This is the time that an intercessor must be prepared to wait on God in order to be ushered into the deeper spiritual realm no matter how long the wait. This is totally in God's timing and His alone.

Chapter Two

INTERCESSION

Wherefore he is able also to save them to the uttermost that come unto God by him, seeing he ever liveth to make intercession for them. Hebrews 7:25

INTERCESSION IS THE act of praying for someone or some situation as assigned by God to pray for that person, place, or situation in a particular way, at a particular time, and/or in a particular place. The Lord Jesus declared, "The Son could do nothing of Himself, but only what He seeth the Father do." John 5:19. So He would heal the sick, raise the dead, cast out demons, and set the captives free. When He was preparing to leave the earth, the Lord Jesus told us that if we believe on Him, we would be able to do the same works that He did and even greater works because He was going back to the Father. The scripture reads, "Verily, verily, I say unto you, He that believeth on me, the works that I do shall he do also, and greater works, than these shall he do, because I go unto my Father." John 14:12. Because we have received Him and believe on His name, we were given the power to become sons of God. Now as sons of God, we have been given access to come boldly before the throne of God, and God has sent the Spirit of His Son into our hearts causing us to also receive the Spirit of adoption giving us the right to call God our Father. So, it is high time that God's people wake up and take what is rightfully ours. It's time to step into what Jesus has set in place for us with His very life. It is time for us to stop approaching God as beggars but as His children in the boldness of the Holy Spirit. For we have been made sons of God by the receipt of the Lord Jesus Christ as our savior; therefore, it is definitely time for the body of Christ to stop trying to be and pray politically correct and be His children and pray the Word of God correctly. There is a dying world out there that is desperately looking for what we have to offer. Intercession requires us to be filled with the same strength and boldness that Jesus exhibited. Because we have been born again and called to intercession, we have been equipped with this strength and boldness via the Holy Spirit. Our focus must be to please God and God alone. The Lord Jesus Christ never tried to please the world. He pleased only the Father. In order to be the intercessor that God requires, we cannot have or be ruled by fear in any area. We must allow God to totally immerse us in Himself in order to enter into intercession. The majority of the time, this kind of prayer is strategic, but there will also be times when God will, simply, tell us just to pray in general. Similarly, there will be times we will know what and when to pray on behalf of another because of a strong urge or a compelling from God to seek Him on their behalf. Although, the sudden desire or knowledge of whom to pray for can be explicit, it still requires a deeper seeking of God in order to ascertain the exact nature of the prayer. This deeper seeking of God could require fasting or just spending several hours or days with God to receive more understanding.

Intercession is not something we just decide to do—it is our calling, our reason for being. No one can enter into true intercession without actively pursuing and developing an intimate relationship with God. How can you effectively pray the heart of God when you don't know the heart of God? Spending time reading the word of God and spending time in prayer every day create and develop our relationship with God. Intercession can only be maintained through the following life disciplines: relationship, purification, consecration, holiness, and obedience as well as possessing a reverential fear of God.

Relationship: An on-going current relationship with Jesus is a must for all intercessors. Just as you would develop a relationship with a person that you love by spending as much time with them as possible to get to know them, this is the same thing that we have to do with God. When we are getting to know someone, we talk to them, and in turn, they talk to us as we listen. As stated earlier, this can be accomplished in daily prayer and fellowship as well as in daily Bible reading. We can also develop our relationship with God by making sure to be a part of a Bible believing, Holy Ghost filled church where we can participate in the worship of God and receive Bible teaching.

Purification: In developing purification, we must be willing to allow the Holy Spirit to develop our faith. The development of our faith is a process. A process that can be very painful and tedious, dependent upon how willing we are at allowing God to have His way. We must be filled with the Holy Spirit, and be filled with faith. Our hearts are purified by faith. The scripture reads, "And God which knoweth the hearts, bare them witness, giving them the Holy Ghost, even as he did unto us; And put no difference between us and them, purifying their hearts by faith." Acts 15:9. We must come before God with clean hands and a pure heart. We must purify our souls by obeying the truth through the Spirit unto unfeigned love of the brethren. We must also see that we love one another with a pure heart, fervently. The scripture reads, "Seeing ye have purified your souls in obeying the truth through the Spirit unto unfeigned love of the brethren, see that ye love one another with a pure heart fervently;" 1 Peter 1:22

Consecration: To live a consecrated life, we must be dedicated to God's service by presenting our bodies as a living sacrifice, holy acceptable unto God which is your reasonable service. We must not be unequally yoked together with unbelievers. There should be no fellowship between righteousness and unrighteousness. There should be no communion between light and darkness. The scripture reads, "Be ye not unequally yoked together with unbelievers; for what fellowship hath righteousness with unrighteousness? And what communion hath light with darkness." 2 Corinthians 6:14.

Holiness: It is the very essence of God and the requirement is for us to be holy as He is holy. We are commanded to yield to righteousness which is unto holiness. The scripture reads, "For as ye have yielded your members servants to uncleanness and to iniquity unto iniquity; even so now yield your members servants to righteousness unto holiness." Romans 6L19. This can be accomplished only by remaining in the presence of God and being filled with the Holy Spirit of God. The scripture reads, "But as He which hath called you is holy, so be ye holy in all manner of conversation." 1 Peter 1:15

Obedience: Without obedience, there can be no ministry of intercession. We have to be obedient to the Word of God. "Jesus answered and said unto him, if a man love me, he will keep my words and my Father will love him, and We will come unto him and make our abode with him. He that loveth me not keepeth not my sayings and the word which ye hear is not mine, but the Father's which sent me." John 14:23–24. There can be no receiving anything from God if we walk in disobedience. As a parent, this is the exact same way we deal with our children in the natural. Even if we greatly desire to bless our children, we will not and cannot bless them in the midst of disobedience because we love them. God greatly desires to always answer our prayers, but sometimes our disobedience keeps the answer from coming even when we need it the most. Disobedience will block and/or hold up answers to our prayers.

Reverential Fear: The fear and reverence of God is an integral part of the ministry of intercession. Any seasoned saint will attest, an arrogant, prideful stance before God will get you nowhere in the kingdom of God. This will only allow you to keep knocking your head against a brick wall. "The fear of the Lord is the beginning of knowledge; but fools despise wisdom and instruction." Proverbs 1:7. "The fear of the Lord is the beginning of wisdom: a good understanding have all they that do His commandments: His praise endureth forever." Psalm 11:10.

Chapter Three

THE MINISTRY OF INTERCESSION

"And he that searcheth the hearts knoweth what is the mind of the Spirit, because he maketh intercession for the saints according to the will of God." Romans 8:27

HE MINISTRY OF intercession is so much more than just bragging to our sisters and brothers on the quantity of time or the number of hours we spend in our prayer closets. The ministry of intercession is a God calling, and a God mandate to give oneself to praying, interceding, and speaking life into the body of Christ. If we are called, we must be qualified to stand before God to intercede on behalf of another or others, and if we're called, we must be qualified to take authority in the spiritual realm on behalf of another or others. In the ministry of intercession, we are called to live, breathe, eat, and think like our Lord and Savior Jesus Christ. If called to the ministry of intercession, our duties are not complete when we step out of our prayer closets. It's just beginning. We have been misled into thinking that an intercessor is supposed to spend endless hours before God begging Him to intervene on the behalf of others. All of that is fine and good, but God is not going to waste time redoing what He's already done. We are supposed to emerge from our prayer time with instruction, direction, wisdom, and strength to go and take that authority that has already been given to us and use it in our perspective territories. He's waiting for us, at some point, to realize that we have been given the authority in Jesus' name to call into being whatsoever or speak to whatever we desire in faith with results. We love to quote the scripture where Jesus tells us that if we believe on Him, we shall do the same works as He did and even greater works shall we do. The scripture reads, "Verily, verily, I say unto you, he that believeth on me, the works that I do shall he do also; and greater works than these shall he do; because I go unto my Father." John 14:12. But if we reread the Bible, we will see that, yes, Jesus did spend quite a bit of time in prayer, but when He emerged from prayer with His instructions, He did not just take a seat and wait on God, but He immediately began to take authority by commanding evil forces, casting out demons, and calling things in from the unseen realm into the seen realm. This is what we're supposed to do as well in order to fulfill the prophesy of Jesus to do the same works as He. It does not seem to be much available current teachings on the ministry of intercession, and yet, the ministry of intercession is the most powerful ministry in the kingdom of God. I believe this because the ministry of intercession was a part of every called man and woman of God in the Bible. Due in large part to some long held misconceptions about the ministry of intercession, we have gotten way off track and must be re-educated as to God's definition of the ministry of intercession. I have learned that the assignment of intercession is a direct mandate from God Himself. All of the saints of the Bible were called to stand in the gap regardless of their respective titles. I believe every successful ministry/minister was first called to the ministry of intercession and the ministry of worship. If we take a deeper look, we will see that it matters not what the current office or final designated calling, every minister has to be an intercessor, whether for their congregation, family members, or for their own ministry, they must be willing to accept the call of intercession and worship if they are to succeed in their ministries.

Amazingly, this ministry is a behind the scenes ministry. This ministry is capable of reaching around the world at any time and from anywhere—if need be. Only the minister of intercession, God, and the enemy will know about it. This ministry is revealed and made manifest in the scripture in several ways by many of God's prophets throughout the Bible. For example, the ministry of intercession is alluded to in the book of Genesis when Abraham interceded for Lot and his family. Abraham had to fulfill the role of an intercessor in order to save Lot, his nephew. He interceded before God for Lot and his family when God was forced to send His angels to destroy Sodom and Gomorrah. Abraham prayed on Lot and his family's behalf when God revealed to him that He planned to destroy Sodom and Gomorrah because of the grievous sins of those cities. Abraham began immediately to speak to God concerning the souls that were in those cities. The Bible says in the book of Genesis that he drew near to God to begin interceding. The scripture reads, "Abraham drew near, and said, "Wilt thou also destroy the righteous with the wicked? Peradventure there be fifty righteous within the city; wilt thou also destroy and not spare the place for the fifty righteous that are therein?" Genesis 18:32–33 Abraham would not relent until God promised him as it shows in the Bible that He would not destroy Sodom and Gomorrah for even ten righteous people. Then, again, we are taught in the scripture that Moses was required to intercede on behalf of the children of Israel. Moses was an intercessor for the children of Israel when their disobedience provoked God to anger.

Exodus 32. Further in scripture, intercession is demonstrated with the prophet Samuel who constantly interceded on behalf of the children of Israel during his ministry. As we study the Bible, we realize that the ministry of intercession was also an integral part of all of the major and minor prophets' lives such as Jeremiah, Isaiah, Ezekiel, Nehemiah, Amos, and many more. Solomon also operated in the ministry of intercession when he prayed for God to bless the people in the book of 1 Chronicles. As we see in the Bible, intercession has always been a very focal and powerful part of the call to the ministry. The prophets Isaiah, Jeremiah, Ezekiel, and Daniel just to name a few could all have been called intercessors as a substantial amount of their time in the ministry was used to stand in the gap before God for the people. As we know Jesus interceded for us with His very life and still intercedes for us daily. The scripture reads, "It is Christ that died, yea rather, that is risen again, who is even at the right hand of God, who also maketh intercession for us." Romans 8:34.

By studying the scripture from the Old Testament to the New Testament, we realize that the calling to the ministry of intercession was not and is not an easy calling. This calling is especially hard because it calls for the flesh to be completely annihilated. Every one of the prophets and even Jesus Himself had to put their desires and their wants aside—not just for a while but forever. This total dedication to the lifestyle of intercessor is portrayed by the lives of Anna and Simeon who were intercessors and operated in that capacity as is revealed in the book of Luke. They dedicated their entire lives to the ministry of intercession. God used Anna, the prophetess, and Simeon to pray or intercede for the Messiah to come. Simeon was a just and devout man that lived in Jerusalem. He was waiting for the consolation of Israel. The Bible states that the Holy Ghost was upon him, and the Holy Ghost revealed to him that he would not see death until he had seen the Lord's Christ. The Spirit of God led him to the temple just when Jesus' parents brought him to Jerusalem to present him to the Lord as the law of the Lord required. Simeon saw Jesus and held him in his arms and blessed God and blessed Jesus, Mary and Joseph as well. He also prophesied over them as well.

According to scripture, Anna was a widow of eighty-four years, who did not leave the temple, but served the Lord with fastings and prayers day and night. Anna, was a prophetess from the tribe of Asher. She was given in marriage by her father Phanuel, but became a widow after only seven years. After the death of her husband, she spent the rest of her life in service to the Lord. So, likewise, Anna was also at the temple on that day Jesus' parents brought him to the temple to be dedicated to God and likewise gave thanks unto the Lord God for Jesus and spoke to all that looked for the coming of the Lord.

Intercession is an integral part of the body of Christ. The Bible admonishes us to pray without ceasing. The most important and greatest example of the ministry of intercession is with our Lord Jesus Christ. Jesus had and has the ultimate ministry of intercession. First of all, He came to stand in the gap for us by dying in our place, and He washed away our sins in His own blood. He, then, made a way for us to have access to the throne of God the Father. He also possesses the keys of hell and death. And even now, He is forever interceding for us before the Father.

Amazingly, this ministry can be performed anywhere and at any time. This ministry does not require a building or an audience. This ministry does not require travel—at least not in the natural. Nor does this ministry require the permission of anyone other than God. This ministry does, however, require your total surrender and availability twenty-four hours a day. This ministry can cause monumental changes in lives, places, and circumstances. This ministry can cause leaders to make critical and wise decisions in the midst of confusing circumstances. And yet, this ministry can remove confusion and bring peace to a situation.

This ministry demands certain requirements to be met by the minister. If you have been called to the ministry of intercession, you have been called to a ministry that requires you to be on call day and night. We are required to keep ourselves from all and anything that would contaminate or dull our hearing. We are required to allow God to continually groom and prune us. We are required to lay down our ideas and take up His. We are required to learn of Him, and then exhibit Him and His heart to His people. This ministry dictates that we prefer others before ourselves. It dictates that we love our enemies. It dictates that we pray for those who persecute us. It dictates that we take up our crosses and follow Jesus. It dictates that we take up no offense. It dictates that we study the Word of God daily. It dictates that we walk in love with everyone, especially the body of Christ. A minister of intercession must never, ever seek the spotlight or fame, but must seek anonymity. God is looking for well-trained, dead saints to fulfill this call to ministry of intercession!

Chapter Four

QUALIFYING TO COMMAND THE FORCES

"The LORD is nigh unto them that are of a broken heart and saveth such as be of a contrite spirit." Psalm 34:18

"For thou desirest not sacrifice; else would I give it: thou delightest not in burnt offering. The sacrifices of God are a broken spirit: a broken and a contrite heart, O God thou wilt not despise." Psalm 51:16–17.

I F WE ARE going to be used of God in today's culture, we have to purposely set aside some serious God time and prayer time for strength and for instruction. We are in the greatest battle of our lives, and we have to be ever watchful of the tricks and traps of the enemy. For so many years, we have been overloaded with teachings on the subject of claiming what is rightfully ours in the kingdom of God, but what we have not been taught is the process by which we are to lay hold of this claim. Of course, we're supposed to claim what's ours, but we have to stop and realize that just because it belongs to us, and we even declare it's ours, does not guarantee that the current holder or rather the

20

enemy will, readily, relinquish it to us. We are going to have to kick down the door and go in and wrangle it out of his evil hands. So, with that being said, we must realize that we have to do some serious preparation. We have to begin by being properly armed by appropriating the correct weapons, become very familiar with the weapons, and learn how to use the weapons. Only then can we defeat the enemy, and finally, go in and possess what's rightfully ours. This all starts with attaining and developing our relationship with the Lord. We cannot afford to become lukewarm in our relationship with the Lord. We have to purposely work at keeping our relationship with the Lord current, passionate, and pleasing to Him. We are clearly living in perilous times. These are the times that we have read about over the years but thought we would never have to see come to pass in our lifetime. Unfortunately, we who are in the earth at this juncture in time are witnessing with our own eyes what we've read about for so many years. Consequently, the body of Christ is in dire need of its prayer warriors like never before. We need to be available to the Lord for Him to be able to call on us to spend time in prayer, in intercessory prayer for His people and for the world even. I admit, in today's culture, the opportunity to become easily distracted is at an all-time high due to the inundation of portable media access. Additionally, it is just as easy to become distracted by being busy with day to day life that we can begin to slowly neglect our prayer time and our time alone with God. We must fight to get back anything that we may have lost in our time with God. We must fight this fight with everything that's within us. When we look around at the condition of the world, we can begin to feel overwhelmed. But, in those times, we have to remember that the Word of God tells us that when sin abound, the grace of God do much more abound. We have to remember that we are to cast all of our cares upon the Lord because it is He that loves us. We have to remember that the Bible teaches us to not to grow weary in well-doing. We are to keep ourselves in a position to go to God as the saints of old and say, here am I God, send me. It is time to seek God as never before. It is time to go after lost souls as never before. It is time to pray for the body of Christ as never before. Let's stand up and be counted for the kingdom of God. We have been put in the earth for such a time as this. Let's use the authority that we have been given by Almighty God in the name of His Son Jesus Christ. Let's get into position so that God can use us as He sees fit and whenever He sees fit.

God is looking for saints that know they are called to intercessory prayer and are ready to accept their calling. Anyone who has a problem being awakened at three o'clock in the morning and views such as a personal affront and an unwelcomed infringement upon their best sleep time might not be qualified to be an intercessor. I make this statement because, in my experience, this is frequently the time of day that God the Holy Spirit has chosen to speak. What I am trying to convey is that we, as Christians, must remember some things! Things that are defined in scripture that tells us that we are called in the Lord, being servants. The Scripture reads,

> "Let every man abide in the same calling wherein he was called. Art thou called being a servant? Care not for it: but if thou mayest be made free, use it rather. For he that is called in the Lord, being a servant, is the Lord's freeman: likewise also he that is called, being free, is Christ's servant. Ye are bought with a price; be not ye the servants of men." 1 Corinthians 7:21–24.

We all need to and must ask God to give us what we need spiritually, mentally, and physically in order to do what we have been called to do. No, I never said it would be easy to bring our bodies under subjection, but I do say that it can be done and must be done if God has called us to be the ones to go before; to stand in the gap, and, yes, to get out of our comfortable beds at the crack of dawn, if need be. Frankly, sometimes the older we become in the Lord, the more He has to prompt us to be obedient. I believe this is so because of a very unattractive attribute of human nature that leads us to take people and/or things for granted. I would not advise anyone to take this stance with God. I can tell you from personal experience, it is a very, very dangerous one.

There are a lot of voices speaking to us in the world today, and if we do not know the voice of God, we too will be led in the wrong direction as has so many others who allowed themselves to listen to all the very confusing voices speaking at us today. In both observation and experience, it appears that in the intercessory prayer qualifying process, God always began with teaching us to recognize His voice whenever and wherever He is speaking and through whomever He is speaking. The scripture reads, "My sheep hear my voice, and I know them, and they follow me." John 10:27. This recognition process cannot be achieved via a flesh participatory process but by a spiritual one only. In other words, we can only recognize the voice of God in our born again spirits. Just as we that worship God can only worship Him in spirit and in truth, we can only truly hear Him in spirit and in truth. The scripture reads, "God is a Spirit: and they that worship him must worship him in spirit and in truth." John 4:24. After being born again, God the Holy Spirit will take us into His Word to learn of Jesus. As we see in the scripture when we observe the life of our Lord in the earth those thirty-three years, we learn that He would always be guided by the Holy Spirit in making every decision. Every word He spoke would be spoken directly from heaven. As it is being manifested today in the lives of many so-called followers of Jesus, we cannot last for very long in our own strength. Evidently, this is par for the course for all who are not led to belief in Jesus Christ by God the Holy Spirit. If it wasn't for the keeping power of the Holy Spirit, there is not a one of us that would be a follower of the Lord Jesus Christ for very long. We, too, would bail out as soon as things didn't make sense to our natural minds or when persecution arose if we were not born again spiritually. Just as this was proven in the scripture, it is still being proven in the same way in the various churches of today. For example, when Jesus was speaking to the crowd concerning eating His body and drinking His blood, the seventy that were following Him left because Jesus' words were offensive to them. Only Peter and the other eleven disciples remained. Although, they did not fully comprehend what the Lord was saying at the time, they were able to hear and trust Him because they belonged to God. What I am saying is that we have to listen and discern what God is speaking to us with our spirits and not with our minds. In order to be able to constantly hear and discern the things of God, we must remain in the spiritual realm at all times. We must be able to declare as Jesus did that we only do what we see our Father doing. For the scripture reads, "But as many as received him, to them gave he power to become the sons of God, even to them that believe on His name". John 1:12. "For as many as are led by the Spirit of God, they are the sons of God.". Romans 8:14.

The following chapters will, in more detail, take us through the steps that I believe God leads each us through in the qualification process to command the forces. I believe He is speaking to all of us who have been called for such a time as this. If we, as intercessors, follow what God is saying and allow God to fill us with the Holy Spirit and do in us what is necessary in order to get us prepared for the job, we will be able to do as Jesus told us to do before leaving the earth. The scripture reads, "The Lord Jesus declared that all who believed on Him would be able to ask the Father for anything in His name and the Father would hear and answer. And they that are Christ's have crucified the flesh with the affections and lusts. If we live in the Spirit, let us also walk in the Spirit." Galatians 5:24–25. In qualifying to command the forces, the most important segment of that qualification sequence is getting ourselves into the position to allow God to take us through the process. Once, we're finally in the position that God requires, we must learn how to resist the temptation to take ourselves out of that position when things start to get crazy. And, believe me, they will get crazy as the process progresses. If we allow God to take us through to the other side, we will no longer be in the position of a victim, but we will be able to take our rightful places as victors in every situation. Our rightful places as the ones in authority and in command in Jesus' name. Although, we might know that we have been called to a particular office in the kingdom of God, there is still a qualifying process that only God Himself can properly grade us on and deem us as being graduated and qualified for His use. Let's read on to see what God wants us to know.

Chapter Five

CHURCH IN TURMOIL

"So that we ourselves glory in the churches of God for your patience and faith in all your persecutions and tribulations that ye endure;" 2 Thessalonians 1:4

HY IS THE church of Jesus Christ experiencing the very same turmoil as the world? The answer is that there are several reasons, but I will only discuss the ones that I believe are the most prevalent and pertinent ones affecting the church at this juncture in our walk with the Lord. I believe the majority of the body of Christ have gotten too relaxed, and we have let our passion for the Lord cool down to a simmer instead of being at a boil. I believe that a large number of saints are also living under the misconception that once we become born again, we are exempt from the kind of attacks that the enemy is unleashing on the world by default. This relaxed state along with the aforementioned misconception are being fueled by a very important but misapplied aspect of the Christian walk—our perspective. The way we perceive the Bible and the Word of God can either set us free or put us in bondage. We have to be very careful that we are led by the written Word of God and not by the ideas of human beings. Unless we let the Bible be our only guide, we will always be totally confused. If we allow anything or anyone other than the Word, itself, to be our foundation, our perceptions will always be misconstrued. A large majority of our Christian brothers and sisters have the mistaken idea that what the saints of old experienced in the earth while serving the Lord has nothing, whatsoever, to do with us today. We look at their lives and think, I'm so glad that we don't have to go through that kind of persecution now. Wrong! As I stated earlier, we, the saints of today have the wrong perception concerning the attacks from the enemy. The average one of us Christians believes deep in our hearts that if God has called and chosen us to be used in the kingdom, we will not ever have to experience any resistance whatsoever. We also have the distorted idea that once we begin to operate in our respective callings, all will be smooth sailing, and by no means will we ever have to experience any suffering today in the kingdom. I really believe that these type of erroneous perceptions are why the body of Christ seem to be less forgiving of our own than the world. If we or any saint do experience any attacks from the enemy, we immediately begin to believe that there is something very wrong with our walks with the Lord. Wrong, again! In actuality, it's just the opposite. In most cases, it really means that we are doing something right. It means that we have gotten the devil's attention.

Sadly, today, most of us do not believe this and when we encounter the least bit of push back from the enemy, we quickly run out of stamina and retreat back to God in tears. As a result, we become offended in God and start to become silent. Unfortunately, this is where the majority of the body of Christ is in this day and time. Granted, the saints of God should not be experiencing attacks from the enemy for the same reason as the unsaved and unchurched world. But we should realize that there will be some battles to fight for which we have already been equipped. Nor should the church be reacting to the attacks in the same way as the world. The saved and Holy Ghost filled saints of God, if attacked, should be attacked for the winning of souls and the healing of sicknesses and the casting out of demons. When Peter and Paul and the other apostles continued the work that the Lord Jesus left for them to do, there was not one instance where the apostles or saints ever fell into illnesses and bondages as the rest of the unsaved people. Their troubles and the threats they encountered were from the Pharisees and others trying to prevent them from continuing the work of the Lord. Just as the saints of old were threatened because of doing good, so should it be for the saints of today. Just as the apostles did, we too are supposed to embrace each attack from the enemy. Each time we are attacked, we should greatly rejoice as the apostles—Peter, James, John, and Paul, etc. did. They counted it a privilege and an honor to suffer for the Lord. They rejoiced and thanked the Lord that they were counted worthy to suffer for the kingdom of God. The scripture reads, "And they departed from the presence of the council, rejoicing that they were counted worthy to suffer shame for His name." Acts 5:41

Yes, I know, this kind of reaction requires a total yielding to the Holy Spirit. The saints of today are far removed from the kind of suffering that the saints of old endured for the kingdom of God. We only want to read about the price that was paid by Peter, James, John, and Paul to further the kingdom of God. As we read the Bible, we observe that every day with the saints of God were not happy, stress free days. In fact, most of their days were filled with threatening's, prison, and even with some of them actually being murdered for doing the work of the Lord. Acts 7

The average Christian is not in love with the person of our Lord Jesus Christ of the Bible, but with our own personal perceptions of Jesus. We do not really trust the Lord as we claim, but we would rather have everything handed to us without having to use our faith. As we know, the Bible teaches us that without faith it is impossible to please God. Hebrews 11:6. So, if we don't please God, we don't get our prayers answered, and we do not get to know God. If we think about it, if we don't know Him, we don't love Him.

In the church, there are not many intercessors or saints that have a thorough working knowledge of God's Word. We must gain knowledge of God's Word in order to gain more knowledge of His heart's desires. We must become more intimate with God in the spirit or through the Spirit, so that our prayers are answered. One very important aspect of getting to know God's Word keeps us more protected from the deadly tricks and traps of the enemy. One of the greatest weapons in the enemy's tool chest is the spirit of pride. We must be very, very, careful to be aware of developing a prideful stance. This is one his most deadly and subtle tools that manifests itself in various ways, and it is one of his favorites that he uses often. The enemy is very clever at using pride as he always devises a stratagem against God's people to transmit this spirit. This spirit of pride is also adeptly used upon the body of Christ and other people in this capacity to cause dissension in our homes, on our jobs as well as in the house of God. We have to guard our thought life, guard our love walk, and guard our time in the Word of God because the Word trumps all. The Word of God combined with love and prayer is our greatest weapon. This combination neutralizes, paralyzes, and stops the enemy in his tracks and causes him to run for cover every time. The more we know the Word of God and about the things of GOD, the more we have to walk a straight line because a praying, Word of God saint is the greatest foe of the enemy. He will try and stop us in any way possible from knowing and utilizing the Word of God. The more we learn about the Word of God, the more we get to know the Father, the Son, and the Holy Spirit; thereby causing us become an even greater threat to the enemy. Because the church has gotten too lazy to seek God for ourselves and are relying on others in the church or even worse, others in the world, we are allowing the enemy to virtually take over the minds of so many unsuspecting people.

Because the church is being quiet on so many pertinent topics affecting the church and world today, we're allowing the enemy to take over to the point of setting up, what I term as being, para worlds for some people. My definition of this as I have observed and witnessed is when the enemy has, literally, taken over the thoughts of some people to the point of affecting their reasoning. They become unable to distinguish real from the imaginary. They are calling right wrong and wrong right—in and out of the church. This takeover of the enemy is so pervasive that the people that are affected are to the point of only hearing the voice of the enemy. Although, they still appear to be participating in normal day to day activities here in the natural, they are really somewhere else in the spirit. The affected people that I have, personally, observed all operate on a very short fuse and often exhibit fits of anger for, apparently, no reason. I'm sure each of us know someone that exhibits this kind of behavior. Because these people are under the influence of the enemy, they perpetrate some of the most heinous crimes to the utter shock of the people that believe they know them personally. Just to be clear, I'm not saying every person that has an anger problem will commit some type of heinous crime. If the church does not speak up and be willing to stand for God through certain persecution, there will be a lot of lost souls whose blood will be required at our hands. The scripture reads,

"When I say unto the wicked, O wicked man, thou shalt surely die, if thou dost not speak to warn the wicked from his way, that wicked man shall die in his iniquity, but his blood will I require thine hand." Ezekiel 33:8.

God is looking for saints that are not concerned with being politically correct, but is concerned with being Word of God correct. He's looking for people that He can point out as He did with Job and know that they will stand. God is looking for saints in the church who will have the same praise in their mouths at all times, whether they're on the mountain top or whether they're in the valley. He's looking for saints that will not cower and run for the hills at the first instance of trouble. God needs faith-filled prayer warriors in the church. He's looking for saints that believe what He said just because He said it. Just because He's God. An intercessor is called to lay down his or her lives as Jesus did so that others can live; Only we are called to do it in the spirit—not in the natural as the Lord Jesus had to do. Intercessors and all saints, especially in the church, are supposed to be carriers of the most infectious thing to ever be loosed in the earth and spread it to all people in the earth. We are called to be carriers of the Holy Spirit of the living God, and we are called to manifest what we're carrying through our love to one another as our Lord and Savior Jesus commanded.

The church must begin to realize that the responsibility is so much greater today because of where we currently are in the world spiritually. The hearts of many have grown cold just as the scripture teaches. People have begun to put more emphasis on the material instead of the spiritual. They have become obsessed with more book knowledge and the acquisition of various degrees more than at any other time in the history of the world. This is done with the pursuit of more and more money as the motivating factor. They aim to make more money which they believe will give them a better quality of life. When in actuality, they are getting into greater and deeper debt and making themselves what the

Bible calls slaves to the lender. Of course, there is nothing wrong with improving oneself and getting a good quality education. What I'm saying is God does not want us to get ourselves into and become overwhelmed by a stronghold of debt which will cause us to not have the freedom to have the life as He's intended for His people. You see, when people are being strangled by debt, they are more likely to compromise in areas that they would not do ordinarily. This brings me to my concern which is people seem to be exchanging God for worldly knowledge and financial wealth. In some instances, the case can be made for the fact that more and more people seem to be forgetting God altogether in their pursuit of more worldly pursuits. This is readily evident in in the very low church attendance across this nation. There are also so many sick people, in and out of the church, and so much depravity going on worldwide. We, the church of God, don't seem to know what to do and are, literally, standing around wringing our hands instead of going on our knees. We are supposed to be the light on the hill shining brightly showing the world the way to real knowledge, real riches, and real joy and peace. We are not supposed to be in as much or more turmoil than the world. We should be the ones setting the standard. The church, surprisingly, have too much concern about what the world thinks of it. We have too much concern about looking strange to the world. News flash! That is exactly what we're supposed to do! We're supposed to be different from the world! Along with those differences, we're supposed to have something to offer that is life altering for their good and betterment. We must not forget both John the Baptist and our Lord Jesus, Himself, who were as different from the world as anyone could be. We are not called to be popular, but we are called to be change makers and influencers for righteousness. When we, the church, begin to care more about what the world thinks of us rather than what God thinks, we have virtually declared the world and its system as our God. And, we all know who it is that is directing and mandating the world's system—Satan. We must read the Word of God for ourselves as to not be duped by the enemy into thinking that we are to be pleasing to the world. Rather, we are supposed to take over the world by spreading the Word and by demonstrating the love of Jesus. There are people looking for what we have, but the light has gotten very, very dim in some cases. The Bible says, if my people who are called by my name shall humble themselves and pray ... I will hear them from heaven ... and heal their land. The scripture reads,

"If my people, which are called by my name, shall humble themselves, and pray, and seek my face, and turn from their wicked ways; then will I hear from heaven, and will forgive their sin, and will heal their land." 2 Chronicles 7:14.

If the statistics are accurate, there are only a few churches that are still putting emphasis on prayer. There are very few that are still making prayer their foundation.

Let's just be frank! A very large majority of the church of Jesus Christ have grown very, very weak and the light that we're supposedly carrying has almost gone out! The average church body have been caught up in the same web of deceit that the enemy has, so cleverly, set in motion to ensnare the unsuspecting world. So many are being deceived into forgetting about or abandoning their God-given uniqueness to follow the dictates of others in the world that appear to be successful. Unfortunately, we, the body of Christ, have also become so engrossed in comparing ourselves with each other and with the world. This is in direct disobedience to the Word of God. The scripture reads, "But they measuring themselves by themselves and comparing themselves among themselves, are not wise." 2 Corinthians 10:12.

As a prime example, in the church, we are more concerned with the number of people that are in attendance in our buildings than we are about showing the love of God to the few or number of people that we currently have because of the size of the congregation that attends pastor so and so's church. We are forgetting that God has never been dependent upon a large number of people in order to do a mighty work in the earth and/or in His people. Don't get me wrong, numbers are good, great even, if they are mixed with God's requirements of reverence, love, submission, and obedience. What I'm saying is God is looking for people whose hearts are perfect toward Him, people that He can use, a church without spot or wrinkle, whether large or small. The Bible teaches us as born again Christians, we are seated in heavenly places in Christ Jesus, and we are ambassadors for Christ in the earth. As the church of God, we must wise up and take seriously our responsibilities as His ambassadors in the earth. The scripture reads,

"But God, who is rich in mercy, for his great love wherewith he loved us, Even when we were dead in sins, hath quickened us together with Christ, (by grace ye are saved.) And hath raised us up together, and made us sit together in heavenly places in Christ Jesus…Now then we are ambassadors for Christ, as though God did beseech you by us: we pray you in Christ's stead, be ye reconciled to God." Ephesians 2:5–6; 2 Corinthians 5:20.

Chapter Six

THE CHURCH AND THE SPIRIT OF OFFENSE

"And then shall many be offended, and shall betray one another, and shall hate one another." Matthew 24:10

IF ACCURATELY RESEARCHED, it will reveal that an astronomical number of destroyed families, empty churches, and broken friendships have been done in by way of the spirit of offense. The spirit of offense has done irreparable damage to the body of Christ worldwide without the affected persons being aware of its deadly participation. The reason that so many of us have been taken down by this spirit is because we did not have the slightest clue as to what was happening. Some of us, years later, are still harboring anger and unforgiveness toward another person or persons that were unwittingly involved in the enemy's diabolical plan. We are looking in the wrong direction at the people instead of at the real culprit which is the devil. It is he that has caused the dissensions, hard feelings, and spiritual wounds. We, as well as the other participants, were merely pawns. Don't ever be surprised at whom or what the enemy will use to try and bring offense. This, offense, is a most deadly tool used by a most deadly enemy. The main reason the enemy is able to unleash the same attacks upon the church as he has so cleverly done in the world is due in large part to this spirit of offense as well as our lack of knowledge as to how and protect ourselves from it. I will go so far as to say offense is the most pervasive, diabolical, destructive, and effective weapon that the enemy has in his arsenal. It has caused more church splits, divorces, and dissolved friendships than any other weapon the enemy has ever used. This weapon is so effective because it is odorless, colorless, tasteless, and invisible. It can be totally undetected, and it hits the bullseye every single time and never ever misses its target. It is also very dangerous because no one other than the affected ones and God will ever know that this spirit is rearing its ugly head.

This spirit, if left alone, will affect every area of our lives because it grows rapidly and sets up strongholds. What I'm saying is that it begins in the heart and is fed with our minds. The enemy will constantly bombard our minds with the memory of the situation or circumstance that created the avenue for the offense to take hold. Each time we think about it and meditate on it, it will grow exponentially. It will influence every decision from the moment of its entry. This spirit is very deceitful and will cause us to feel our strongest when we're actually in our weakest state. It will stunt your spiritual growth. In addition, if we do not recognize and immediately eradicate this spirit, it will stop us dead in our spiritual tracks and slowly begin to take us backwards without our ever realizing it until we're caught up in one of the enemy's webs of deceit. We will begin to lose our sensibilities to the things of God. We will begin to accept and become comfortable with things (sin) that we would have never allowed in before. The enemy will ensure that someone will be available to help us rationalize our feelings and/or our actions. If we do not know what it is or rather have not been trained to recognize it, we will become more and more entangled in its far reaching tentacles. This spirit can hit its target from any distance through any medium. In other words, we cannot prevent this spirit from coming, but we can keep it from taking root and growing. We can send it packing every time it comes a calling.

There is only one way to successfully conquer the spirit of offense when it presents itself. The only way is to immediately recognize it for what it is and then give it to the Lord Jesus Christ. We must never let this spirit linger. I reiterate, it has to be eradicated immediately. This can be accomplished by simply taking and casting all of our cares upon the Lord Jesus Christ just as He asked us to do. We also have to immediately take this spirit to God in the name of Jesus and ask Him to not just remove it but to please replace it with perfect love. This exact sequence is very, very important. Important because we on our own cannot remove this spirit and cannot replace it without the help of God. Important because if the spirit is just simply removed and not replaced, the enemy will have an even easier access the next time it is presented. And, yes, it will be presented again and again. The scripture reads,

"When the unclean spirit is gone out of a man, he walked through dry places, seeking rest, and findeth none. Then he saith, I will return into my house from whence I came out, and when he is come he findeth it empty, swept, and garnished. Then goeth he, and taketh with himself seven other spirits more wicked than himself, and they enter in and dwell there and the last state of that man is worse than the first. Even so shall it be also unto this wicked generation." Matthew 12:43

Unfortunately, the spirit of offense seems to operate at its best in the church and the body of Christ. The average church body does not realize or rather forget that we wrestle not against flesh and blood but against principalities, against powers, against the rulers of the darkness of this world, against spiritual wickedness in high places." Ephesians 6:12-13. This is one of the major reasons that there are so many church splits, divorces, and dissolved friendships in the body of Christ. Some are under the deception that we are fighting people (flesh and blood). The Bible clearly tells us that we are not fighting people, but we're really fighting evil spirits. Until the church/body of Christ understand this truth, it will continue to resemble the defeated world instead of a victorious church as God intended. Because this weapon of the enemy is used at its best in the confines of close intimate relationships, it is very hard to see it coming. Therefore, the enemy always has the element of surprise on his side. That being said, we have to accept that offenses will come and the only protection is our awareness of the spirit of offense and walking in the spirit of love, preferring others above ourselves. Because the effect of the spirit of offense is painful, we tend to be swift in our reaction before thinking things through. We just reciprocate in kind causing this spirit to dig in and take an even stronger hold in our minds. But, if we walk in the love of God at all times, we will be slow to react in kind and consider the other person before ourselves.

An even greater danger of the spirit of offense, if left unchecked and not rooted out by the Word of God, is you cannot be forgiven by God. The scripture reads, "But if ye do not forgive neither will your Father which is in heaven forgive your trespasses. Mark 11:26. If we cannot be forgiven for our sins, then how can we as an intercessor expect our prayers to be heard and answered by God. In other words, if we cannot ever be forgiven for our sins, we will have no recourse, no hope and the enemy would have won on every front. This not only applies to our lives, but applies to the lives of our entire households. There are lots of people refusing to deal with this spirit head on and are reaping the negative rewards personally and spiritually. It has to be confronted and eradicated because it does not just get better but will grow stronger. It can get buried but not better. The problem with this stance is that we have virtually given the enemy control over our lives and the lives of our loved ones. He will have a free pass to push that offense button whenever he chooses to bring that offense back to the top at his discretion. And, believe me, he will push that button often. We must make the choice to set not only ourselves free but our households free as well.

So often, we, the body of Christ, become offended when trials and tribulations come. We feel as if no negativity should come nigh us and begin to question God and be offended at Him. We are forgetting some very pertinent scripture that tells us that it shall rain on the just and the unjust. The scripture reads, "That ye may be the children of your Father which is in heaven; for He maketh His sun to rise on the evil and on the good and sendeth rain on the just and on the unjust." Matthew 5:45. The scripture also reads, "Many are the afflictions of the righteous; but the LORD delivereth him out of them all." Psalms 34:19. In other words, God did not promise us that we would not experience any suffering, but He did promise to always be with us, and He promised to deliver us from all adversity. I'm not saying we're supposed to enjoy the trials and tribulations, but I am saying we're supposed to count it all joy by remaining faithful, prayerful, and worshipful during the various trials and tribulations. In fact, James tells us in the scripture that we're supposed to count it all joy when we fall into divers temptations. There is only one way that we can count it as joy when dealing with the various life situations, circumstances, and hardships and that is to be in and remain in Christ Jesus. This is accomplished when we cast all of our cares upon Him and lean not to our own understanding.

Chapter Seven

THE CALL TO INTERCESSION

"Let every man abide in the same calling wherein he was called." 1 Corinthians 7:20.

"Thou therefore endure hardness, as a good soldier of Jesus Christ. No man that warreth entangleth himself with the affairs of this life, that he may please him who hath chosen him to be a soldier." 2 Timothy 2:3–4

INTERCESSORY PRAYER IS more needed at this time in the earth than at any other time since the foundation of the world. This is being witnessed in each and every place in the earth and by each and every person that is in a position to be cognizant of the spiritual condition of the nations. We all are bearing witness to the fact that we are, indeed, experiencing those perilous times that the Bible teaches us would come about in the last days. The scripture reads,

"This know also, that in the last days perilous times shall come. For men shall be lovers of their own selves, covetous, boasters, proud, blasphemers, disobedient to parents unthankful, unholy, without natural affection, trucebreakers, false accusers, incontinent, fierce, despisers of those that are good, traitors, heady, highminded, lovers of pleasures more than lovers of God; having a form of godliness denying the power thereof: from such turn away." 2 Timothy 3: 1–4.

As I look around as well as listen to various news reports, I can attest that we are, most certainly, experiencing some things that are letting us know that we are needed more now than at any other time in history to take up our crosses and follow Jesus. Like never before, I firmly believe that we are now experiencing all of those things that the apostle Paul so accurately detailed in his epistles more than two-thousand years ago. Many people's hearts are turning cold, many are walking in fear to the point of having to be medicated to make it from one day to the next. Many people are so spiritually confused just as the scripture foretold. Many are so greedy for gain that they will do anything to get money, etc., even people in the church. So, yes, this is a time like no other in our life time, and we, desperately, need intercessory prayer and the healing, deliverance, and blessing of God.

When we're called to the ministry of intercession, the enemy recognizes the call on us long before we do. In fact, he's always known who we were and that is why we've been the recipient of such vicious persecution and attacks from the enemy over the years. This is because there is nothing that frightens the enemy more than an intercessor. He is deathly afraid of the intercessor and will use whatever means he's allowed to try and get us to do something to abort our calling. But, when as intercessors, we know who we are in Christ Jesus and walk in that authority, we will keep the devil up at night. I've heard it said many times, even from the pulpit, that everyone can pray. Yes, that is true, but will everybody pray? Will everybody stay in prayer until the answer comes? The position of the intercessor is a very important one and a most strategic one. Our position is a position of prayer, power, and authority in Jesus' name. As an intercessor, we possess unique capabilities given to us by God to bring down every plan, plot, and scheme of the enemy through prayer and by taking authority in Jesus' name. A God-sanctioned intercessor has the capability to hone in on and target the enemy while pulling down the strongholds of the enemy and foiling the enemy's evil plots. A most amazing feat of the called and sanctioned intercessor is that we can operate in our calling from any physical location. But we can only operate from a particular spiritual location or position. If and when we have been called to the ministry of intercession, we have been called to the most difficult and yet the most powerful and the most rewarding call of any human being. Remember, Jesus, our Lord and Savior is an intercessor. If Jesus had to pray, so do we have to pray and even more so.

Intercessors, because our ministry is behind the scenes, Satan will try and tell us that God is not using us like He's using others. Don't fall for that lie, when, in actuality, God is using us greatly every time we pray for or intercede on behalf of someone. Every time we have interceded on behalf of someone, or spoken a Word from God over or into someone, God is accounting any and all harvests that comes through us for those persons to our accounts. When we are operating in our calling as an intercessor or encourager to someone, we are also touching the ones that will be touched or ministered to or brought into the kingdom by them. I believe all intercessors are encouragers. In the same way as with any office or aspect of ministry, God has set a precedence, if you will, that each and every calling is an important one in the eyes of God. This works the same for every saint that serves and obeys the Lord as is shown in the scripture. In the book of 1 Samuel, Chapter 30: 24-25, God made this abundantly clear through His servant David when he returned to the two hundred men that were too tired to go to battle but stayed behind and watched over their property at the camp. The scripture reads, "But as his part is that goeth down to the battle, so shall his part be that tarrieth by the stuff; they shall part alike. And it was so from that day forward, that he made it a statute and an ordinance for Israel unto this day." God is not unfaithful to forget your service. Hebrews 6:10.

Intercessors, should never worry about the accolades of men, but should just continue to bring our flesh under subjection and just continue to seek to please God. Remember, because God has called us to the ministry of intercession, our warfare is stronger than the average saint. That is also one of the reasons we are so much more hated than other saints. Hated and despised even by supposedly fellow saints and family members alike. Intercessors are the ones that have access to the throne room of God in order to intercede on behalf of others. Again, I want to reiterate how much the ministry of intercession is greatly feared by the enemy.

An intercessor is immediately ushered to the front line in our walk with the Lord. As soon as we understand what our calling is we are not allowed any grace period, we literally learn as we go. As the saying goes, you hit the ground running. We are thrown right into the middle of the fight. The good news is that we have been equipped for the fight from the very foundation of the world. Every aspect of our very lives, from birth until our call, has been a source of preparation or training for us and our ministries.

An intercessor will sustain a multitude of attacks from whoever the devil can use. The attacks are on-going. This is how we will know whether or not we are called to the ministry of intercession. Our ability to withstand and persevere in love is a sure sign that we are an intercessor. That we are someone that God can depend upon. In fact, saints, I believe God orchestrates it so that an intercessor will always have something to pray about. To always have the opportunity to hone our skills, so to speak. When I look back, I can see where God was preparing me and even using me to intercede even before I rededicated my life to Him. An intercessor is in training for the ministry of intercession from birth. Our whole lives and every incident or circumstance is in preparation for being an intercessor. Don't worry, if we are not called to be an intercessor, we will soon know it because a person who is a casual prayer would not be able to survive for an extended length of time—literally.

If we survive and do not give up and do not run away from God in the midst of all the testing, we will be chosen to begin to experience a more intimate relationship with the Lord. We will begin to have access to and experience intercession that will take us into a realm where we can see through the eyes of God. Think with the mind of Christ and have the God kind of love. We will have the mercy of God (he who gives mercy will receive mercy). When chosen of God to the ministry of intercession, then and only then can we be an effective intercessor. The ministry of intercession is somewhat mysterious because it is a behind the scenes ministry. As I said earlier, Intercession is the most powerful ministry. It is the ministry of our LORD and Savior JESUS Christ, "He ever liveth to make intercession for us". Heb.7:25; Ro. 8:34.

Chapter Eight

THE PRICE

"That I may know him, and the power of his resurrection, and the fellowship of his sufferings, being made conformable unto his death;" Philippians 3:10

I'M JUST GOING to be real and straight forward with you concerning the cost for the calling of intercessor in the kingdom of God. The cost very high, and it is a cost that only a select few are willing to pay for any amount of time. I firmly believe that this is the reason the Lord God had to search for a man but could not find any one to intercede on behalf of a city so He would not have to destroy it. The scripture reads, "And I sought for a man among them, that should make up the hedge, and stand in the gap before me for the land, that I should not destroy it: but I found none." Ezekiel 22:33. We all read this scripture and wonder why was it a so difficult for the Lord to find this person. In fact, the scripture goes on to say, He could not find anyone. Wow! I know that all who are reading this right now are saying in their spirits, *if I were there, I would have stood in the gap.* Not so fast! Let's just take a deeper look. I agree, in the overall scheme of things, it is an honor and a privilege to be used of God, whatever the calling. Even though we love being able to serve our

Lord, there are circumstances and situations that will arise to give us pause, and we are even told by the Lord Jesus to stop and be sure. The scripture reads,

"And Jesus said unto him, No man, having put his hand to the plough, and looking back, is fit for the kingdom of God...For which of you intending to build a tower, sitteth not down first, and counteth the cost, whether he have sufficient to finish it? Lest haply after he hath laid the foundation, and is not able to finish it, all that behold it begin to mock him, saying, this man began to build and was not able to finish." Luke 9:62; 14:28–30.

I believe the Lord is asking us to stop and count the cost because it is real lives of real people that are at stake. We have to know for sure whether or not we're called and are committed to go the course. We have an enemy that is, literally, waiting to steal, kill, and destroy. To be sure, whatever our calling, there will always be some type of sacrifice experienced. Eventually, each one of us will encounter a certain situation that will require us to have to make a decision concerning our respective lives or ministries that will either send us forward or backward. In some instances, at the time of making a decision, it will seem like an ordinary situation or decision. Likewise, in other instances, you will know that the decision that you must make is a life changing, life altering, life and death choice. There is no such thing in the life of an intercessor as an inconsequential decision. Every decision and/or every situation is an eternal one. Thereby, the price of a successful ministry of intercession can be higher than most are willing to pay. Most people that are called to intercession are prayer warriors and are used to spending more time than most in prayer and fellowship with the Lord. All of us are fine at the onset of our perspective ministries until we are called to go deeper. Deeper in our obedience, deeper in our self-sacrifice, deeper in our love for our enemies, deeper in our forgiveness for those who

46

trespass against us, deeper in praying for those who are being used by the enemy to persecute us. People who are called to the ministry of intercession are sometimes characterized as fanatics or strange. Intercessors are usually not well received in a lot of social groups because of our unrelenting commitment to integrity, and our required close walk with the Lord. As we accept this call of God to begin operating in the ministry of intercession, we must be prepared to be persecuted from some very surprising arenas and from some very surprising people to the highest degree. We will be persecuted in our homes, in your churches, and on our jobs. The ministry that the enemy hates above all other ministries is the ministry of intercession. Because one of the prices of this ministry require us to cry out to God on behalf of others until we get an answer is very heavy. If God has given us the responsibility to pray for someone or some people, the absence of their physical presence does not preclude us from our responsibility. Our physical and emotional circumstances do not preclude our responsibility before Almighty God. What I'm saying is, if there has been some kind of separation or even a rift in our relationships with some, we are still held accountable and responsible to pray for that person or persons. Consequently, we must get before God and get our hearts and spirits right so that we can pray effectually and sincerely. He will hold us responsible! The bottom line, we must love the Lord enough to want to obey and please Him totally. Don't worry, if He's called you to be an intercessor, He has equipped you to stay the course and pay the price.

A very important aspect concerning the cost or price to succeed in this ministry is the love factor. Walking in love, perfect love, is most pleasing to Him because the scripture teaches that God, Himself, is love. The more readily we accept who we are and what we were created to do, the more we will realize who we are in God and what He has put in us. This God kind of love will make it much easier to die to ourselves and allow us to put others before ourselves as the scripture commands. I'm not going to lie and pretend that walking in this agape love will cause our walk to become pain free. Nor will it take away all of the attacks of the enemy to make it easier to pay the price in order to be able to stand before God on behalf of others. But I can attest to the fact that when we let Him prepare us and fill us with His love, it will make it easier for us to make it through all of the obstacles and attacks to success.

As an intercessor, we must be a person that trusts God to know that we never have to defend ourselves in the natural but only take our authority in the spiritual realm when confronted with the attacks of the enemy—no matter whom the enemy uses. But, another very important cost and lesson that an intercessor must learn is that we do not fight in our own strength but must immediately go before God with everything making sure our hearts are right, then praying for and about that situation. In other words, an intercessor takes everything to God and God will defend. This is not to say that there will never be a time to speak to a natural situation or circumstance in the boldness of the Holy Spirit. This is why we are to always, as much as possible, stay prayed up and in position to be ready to take authority over some situations in the spiritual realm. A fight in the natural and the spiritual realm are two different fights. Because, we, as intercessors have been entrusted with the heart of God in His desire for souls to be brought into the kingdom, we must never, ever fight the enemy in the natural. Ephesians 6:12. For one thing, the enemy would relish this opportunity to cause us to self-destruct. As the scripture teaches, waging any battle in the natural is a guaranteed way to lose every time. We, as intercessors, must always remain cognizant of the fact that we are not battling flesh and blood but evil spirits. You see it, it is our responsibility to pray it in or pray about it—not to preach at it or discuss it with anyone else. As an intercessor, it is imperative that we spend time—lots of time in prayer. We must, also, spend as much time in reading God's Word, the Bible, so that we can not only know God's voice, but His heart so as to prevent being deceived by the enemy.

To be effective for the kingdom of God, we must be sure we're called as this is not a ministry that one Sunday morning, we just decide to try it out for a while. This ministry goes beyond just a Sunday morning or Sunday night or Wednesday night prayer service. This is a lifestyle, a 24 hour a day lifestyle. God expects it and God commands it! There are times when we will have to intercede in the middle of the day and likewise in the middle of the night. There will be times when we can stand down the enemy alone in prayer; then, there are other times when we must come into agreement with a prayer partner. "One can send a thousand to flight, two can put ten thousand to flight." Duet. 32:30. And God will always call an intercessor away from the crowd. In other words, as an intercessor we will, more often than not, be somewhat of a loner. Our very best friend, our most trusted confidant will be the Holy Ghost, as we are not, usually, idle chatterers, but speak with power, with purpose, and in the anointing. We are often misunderstood by family because of our time spent in prayer and alone with God. Our life is prayer. Everything is centered around prayer. As an intercessor, we are like the parent behind the child, the trainer behind the athlete. I believe that there are many saints that are called to the ministry of intercession, but do not realize it because they do not understand what the ministry of intercession is.

Commanding the Forces is also written for those who have been called to the ministry of intercession and are still waiting for God to explain it. It is also written for those of us who are not moving forward in our callings because we have never been taught about intercession or might have ever heard of it before. There are some of us that are wondering what will people think when we tell them what we believe is our calling. Whatever the reason for hesitating, *Commanding the Forces* will bring to light some biblical truths that God has held back for such a time as this. What if I told you that Jesus was and is an intercessor? It is written, "Jesus came to give His life as a ransom for many. He came to die in our place, to pay the price, to go to the cross for us." It is also written, "Jesus ever liveth to make intercession for us." Hebrews 7:25.

When called to the ministry of intercession, we cannot and must not have any soul ties. Be warned though, people will call us anti-social; void of social skills, etc. Just hear from God on the developing and the cultivation of all or any interpersonal relationships. The choosing of and the cultivation of the wrong inner-circle and personal relationships can cause us to begin to compromise and lose our anointing, our ministries, and even our intimacy with God, etc. The Anointing—the very presence of God—must be protected at all times. We must take a lesson from our Lord and Savior Jesus and choose our inner-circles only after prayer and fasting. Even after choosing the twelve, He only shared certain things with the entire group and had an inner circle inside the inner circle, so to speak. At certain times in His ministry or when He was at a critical juncture in His own life, He pulled out a certain three individuals (the same three each time) to share in the particular circumstances. The scripture does not go into full detail as to why that certain trio were always pulled out, but we do know that Jesus was always led by the Father in prayer. He was always totally obedient to the Father. That is exactly what we have to do as well. We must always be led by the Holy Spirit, who is the Spirit of the Father; and the Spirit of Christ. We must also realize that the more we become like the Lord, the greater are our battles. The enemy will not back down because we grow more like Jesus, but we will become able to take authority over him and command him to back off because we've grown more like Jesus.

Chapter Nine

REAL INTERCESSORS

"Moreover as for me, God forbid that I should sin against the Lord in ceasing to pray for you; but I will teach you the good and the right way;" 1 Samuel 12:23

REAL INTERCESSORS ARE the skilled, knowledgeable, and dependable intercessors that successfully inflict sustained, strategic attacks upon the enemy's camp every day. Real intercessors know that it takes consistency to tear down all of the evil strongholds of the enemy. Unfortunately, we have come to the realization that thoroughly trained individuals that can do damage at this level to the kingdom of darkness are scarce. Sadly, today, there are less and less of us saints that know who we are in Christ Jesus, and even less of us that have fully accepted what the Lord Jesus has done for us by His shed blood, crucifixion, death, and resurrection. We, the body of Christ, are in dire need of saints who will pray until he or she gets an answer. We need saints who are Word oriented. We need saints who are bold and fearless. We need saints who are not afraid to take authority over the enemy. We need saints who will call those things that be not as though they were while believing they shall have whatsoever they ask in Jesus' name. Real intercessors are the kind of saints who pray effectual and fervent prayers that get the desired results because of our belief and our application of the Word of God. There are a lot of great pray warriors who will pray for us with all of their might, but there are very few who will stand in the gap for us until they get the desired result—whatever the cost.

There are a significant number of us saints that are comparing our prayer skills to others whom we believe to be the very personification of an accomplished and skilled intercessory prayer warrior. We must never, ever compare our praying skills with others. It's not who has the best oratory or prayer skills, but it's about who's in the right spiritual position to get through to God in order to get prayers answered. It's also about who is filled with the boldness of the Holy Spirit in order to stand and take their rightful, authoritative positions in the earth. A real intercessor does not just pray with fervency when the recipients are in close proximity or the recipients are a close friend or relative or even someone with whom you converse with on a regular basis, but will pray with that same fervency for someone in another state or even in another nation. In fact, I must reiterate, our prayer lives have absolutely nothing to do with any soul ties, whatsoever. We have a mandate from God, and only to God do we seek to be pleasing. Yes, we love God's people and must walk in that love; otherwise, we could not be used of God, but we do not seek to please people, ever. Because of the authority that have been given to us as intercessors in the name of the Lord Jesus Christ, we are constantly on watch listening for instructions and promptings from the Holy Spirit. Because of the intense persecution, we have to always be cognizant to remember that if we are born again and filled with the Holy Spirit, we have eternal life and will never die spiritually because the God Head (God the Father, God The Lord Jesus Christ, and God the Holy Spirit) who lives in us cannot die. God is the God of the living and not the God of the dead. The scripture reads, "God is the God of the living, not the dead." Luke 20:38.

Likewise, in the natural, I believe when we are in total obedience to God and fulfilling our callings, we will not depart from our earthly bodies before our time. The scripture reads, Jesus said, "if you have seen Me, you have seen the Father also." John 14:9. In addition, Jesus said, "he that believeth in me shall never die." John 11:26. I shall give him eternal life.

Real intercessor are the saints that are willing to serve with a selfless, self-sacrificing spirit and mindset. This ministry requires us to lay down our lives in order to be alive in Jesus. We must live this life of self-denial by practicing putting others before ourselves. We must lay down our own agendas and take on the Lord Jesus' agenda. We must be willing to have our own Gethsemane experience saying, Father, in the name of Jesus, nevertheless, not as I will, but as thou wilt, Matt. 26:39. The majority of the time only we, the intercessor, and God will know what is going on in our respective ministries. We must become the type of person that does not care who gets the credit as long as God gets the glory. When we are called to the ministry of intercession, it means that we are called to a subservient walk or role in the kingdom of God. This means that we have to be aware of our flesh. This will keep us from falling prey to the enemy and enable us to be pliable to the will and Word of God. Also, this will enable us to more readily say, *Lord have your way in me*, not just with lip service, but with pure hearts. In addition, we will be able to walk in perfect love (Agape love, the love of God), and to be able to live in and display the fruit of the Spirit so that God can use us mightily. The fruit of the Spirit is the personality of God and must be ours as well. The scripture reads, "But the fruit of the Spirit is love, joy, peace, longsuffering, gentleness, goodness, faith, meekness, temperance." Galatians

5:22–23. Again, the bulk of our ministry as an intercessor will and must consist of our being content to watch from afar as our prayers are being answered. In other words, we're not to seek any accolades for what God is doing through us as He and He alone will get the glory. As it is written, since we are crucified with Christ it is not us who lives but Christ who lives in us. The scripture reads, "I am crucified with Christ: nevertheless I live, yet not I, but Christ liveth in me." Galatians 2:20.

The spiritual warfare of an intercessor is tremendous, but God will give us the strength to prevail. Notwithstanding, there is something very valuable that I have learned in that there are times that the Lord will allow us to go through certain situations, I mean heavy situations in order to let us know, exactly, what we have on the inside. Believe it or not, I think it is good to be made aware of who we really are. For instance, we can never really know for sure what we truly believe until we're put in certain predicaments and/or situations that will reveal our true qualities. As we maneuver our way through, then and only then will we know who we really are and what we really believe. There's nothing like difficult and stressful life situations to reveal our true characteristics. During those times, we will find out, for sure, whether or not we believe what we've been claiming to believe. We will, also, discover whether or not we'll go to God or away from God in those times. We might be very surprised at what we will discover about ourselves and what is really deep, deep down on the inside. Sometimes, we might even be surprised positively, and at other times, we just might have some things brought to the surface that require quite a bit more attention. As it was with the Lord and the Apostles, as it will be and is with us and the Lord.

I am also learning that sometimes the life of one called to be an intercessor can be an even more lonely, misunderstood one than ever imagined. In my experience, a major portion of an intercessor's time will be spent alone in the presence of God. We will have to walk alone a lot, especially those of us that try and walk uprightly before God, and live a life of integrity. As an intercessor, we must desire God more than we desire anything else or anyone else. "It is written, And ye shall seek me, and find me, when ye shall search for me with all your heart." Jeremiah 29:13. An intercessor is a person of unmovable, unshakeable faith. We must know (eat, sleep, drink) the Word. We must practice our faith at the leading of the Holy Spirit. We must know God's heart by, consistently, reading the Word and listening in prayer. We must realize and know how the enemy brings a lie, and know, whatever the packaging he uses, it is still a lie if it does not line up with God's Word. John 8:44. The enemy can perpetrate lies in various ways—by dreams, by thoughts, through people, through circumstances, and/or through whatever and wherever the enemy can find an opening. As an intercessor, we must always be on guard and not let the lie or lies of the enemy ever become strongholds or rather something that we would meditate upon. We must immediately cast the lie or lies down by the Word of God as Jesus did—It is Written!! 2 Corinthians 10:4–5; Matthew 4:4. Additionally, we must do whatever it takes—fast, pray, seek, knock, ask to get to that place of unmovable, unshakable faith in order to succeed in this ministry!

We intercessors are usually hidden from the world—sometimes even from ourselves—until God brings or calls us forth. Because we are behind the scenes, we and our ministries are almost always misunderstood by others. As an intercessor, we are called to be people who have to learn to withstand some gruesome attacks from the enemy. Incredibly enough, the most gruesome, awful, and vicious attacks do not just come through and by the world, but through the church as well—from those who are professing Jesus Christ as Lord and Savior.

As intercessors, we are, naturally, worshipers and exhorters of the Most High God. We must practice praying in the spirit every day. As we pray in tongues, we must take the time to listen to the Holy Spirit. We do not just pray and go, but we pray and listen before we go. We are to be steadfast and immovable, and we must not be the ones who easily gives up. As an intercessor, we are aware that we must walk by faith and not by sight in order to receive instruction from God. We must worship God in spirit and truth, and we cannot worship God without knowing who He is. To worship God in spirit is accomplished through the Holy Spirit and to worship God in truth is accomplished through the Word of God—His Word is truth. The Holy Spirit is the Spirit of truth. The Holy Spirit lets us know who God is, makes Jesus more real to us, and always points to Jesus. The Word of God takes us into the truth of God. We have to be filled with Holy Spirit to know who God is because God is a spirit. When we worship in spirit and in truth, we are ushered into a realm far beyond the natural realm into a place that can only be reached through and by way of the Holy Spirit.

We, as intercessors must be totally dependent upon God with every aspect of our lives. I believe the majority, if not all, of God's intercessors will not look like the type of person most people would expect, or even look like someone you would choose out of the crowd to pray for you. I, also, believe this is deliberate on God's behalf because God has and is purposely hiding them for His own time and use. Somehow, the church has been deceived into judging a person's relationship with God by looking on the outward appearance or the outward circumstances when God's Word clearly states just the opposite in the book of 2 Samuel. The scripture reads, "For the LORD seeth not as man seeth; for man looketh on the outward appearance, but the LORD looketh on the heart." 2 Samuel 16:7. People have been deceived into thinking that stuff (material things) equate to great faith or represent a great relationship with God. Yes, God does bless materially, but that is not or should not be the Christian spiritual measuring stick--so to speak. If that was the case, every drug dealer, movie actor, sports player, business owner, etc. would, automatically, be classified as being saved or blessed of God and does not require anyone to pray for them. The average intercessor cannot be discerned by their outward appearance as they are God's secret weapons.

Again, I stress that as an intercessor, we must never, ever expect and/or look for any recognition or pats on the back from human beings. Only God will reward us for our service to the kingdom of God. We, intercessors are, most often, persons of extreme compassion and mercy. We are readily willing and obedient to the Lord and relish praying when and wherever prompted of the Holy Spirit to do so. This is without knowing who or why most of the time; while at other times we will know exactly what and who to pray for. We must be keenly aware of the wiles of the enemy at all times. In order to stay grounded, we must not only consume the Word of God daily but supplement the Word with other Christian based materials as prompted by the Holy Spirit. In addition, we must be under a church covering

We have to be strong and courageous, and we must be tenacious fighters. We must always know when to use that strength and in which direction to point that strength as led by God. We must know who to fight (who the enemy is) as the body of Christ has been duped into battling each other instead of evil spirits. We must be able to hear God's voice at all times, and we must be obedient to the voice of God (explicitly and expediently). I must reiterate, an intercessor must walk in perfect love and faith! As walking in perfect love and faith is an absolute must to be pleasing to and used of God! We must be someone that God can trust, we must be someone we can trust, as well as be someone that other people can trust, mostly, because of the power that has been entrusted to us by God.

As an intercessor, we must be very careful that we are seeing through the eyes of God. We must never lean to our own understanding in the judgement of people and of various situations. We must always remember to seek the Lord in all things and in all situations concerning people—especially His people. We must do unto others as we would have them do unto us. We are to never, ever call bad good and good bad. In order to be sure what God calls good or bad, we have to let the Bible set that standard and not our own ideas or the ideas of others. We must be very careful of what comes out of our mouths as our words carry power because of who lives inside of us. Remember, "Be not deceived; God is not mocked: for whatsoever a man soweth, that shall he also reap." Galatians 6:7 Whatever kind of seed is sown, is the kind of harvest that will be reaped. For instance, if a parent sows a seed of righteousness and holiness, the next generation will produce a harvest of holiness and righteousness. It will also work in the opposite way. If someone sows evil and destruction, they will reap evil and destruction as will their next generation. Whatever you sow, it shall be returned to you. Everything we do and say is a seed being sown. As it is with a farmer so it is with our lives. Each time a farmer plants a crop, he sows seed. He never sows just one seed, he sows multiple seeds all of his farming life and reaps a harvest from every seed whether good or bad. The harvest from those seeds that are sown is always much, much more than the actual seeds that were sown. So, lets sow the love of God to His people and to the world. If our hearts are after God, then we will love what and who God loves.

If we have been called of God to be an intercessor, then God has equipped us to walk in everything that is required to fulfill this calling. It is up to us to get into position for the things in us to be made manifest in due time. An intercessor is supposed to be able to take some hits that the average Christians are not able to withstand. As an intercessor, we will be trusted by God to enter into places in the spiritual realm not open to many others due to the price that has to be paid. We will be given the authority over the enemy for others—even without them knowing it.

If we're an intercessor, we've been targeted by the enemy from day one. I mean from our very earliest of memories, I'm sure we can all recall some things that have happened in our lives that we now know to be attacks from the enemy. Even as we're reading this our memories are being triggered to recall several things that have happened to us that could have taken us out. But by the grace of God, we made it. You see, the closer it gets to the enemy losing his strongholds in our lives, the more intensive his attacks will become.

As we know, because our very lives are training for the ministry of intercession, there is no, actual, grace period. After being called, we intercessors are immediately ushered to the front line. As soon as we understand what our calling is, we are not allowed any down time to ponder our calling, we literally learn as we go being totally dependent upon God. As the saying goes, *we hit the ground running.* We are thrown right into the middle of the fight. The good news is that we have been equipped for the fight from the very foundation of the world. Also, our very lives from birth until our call, have been preparing us for our call. The enemy will always try and stop us; therefore, as intercessors, we will sustain a multitude of attacks from whoever the devil can use. The attacks are on-going. This is how we will know whether or not we're really called to the ministry of intercession. Our ability to withstand and persevere in love is a sure sign that we're intercessors. That we're someone that God can depend upon.

We, as intercessors, are supposed to live a life of consecration, separation, holiness, and purification in order to always be in the position for God to use us. As an intercessor, we must have pure hearts and clean hands. We must be trustworthy and people of integrity not only to fulfill our calling, but we must be someone God can trust with His heart as God is entrusting us with inside information that others are not yet privy to. This is a big, big deal to God. As intercessors, we're also trusted to walk in the authority of the name of the Lord Jesus Christ every day and in every situation. In order for an intercessor to walk in that authority, we must exercise, manifest, and operate every aspect of our lives in and by the Word of God. This is why we're expected to know the Word of God, love the Word of God, learn and hear the voice of God and then pray the will of God. An intercessor is the one who God uses to forge a path in prayer for others to go through. As an intercessor, we are called to not only share in the power of the Lord Jesus' resurrection' and the fellowship of His suffering, but also share in His persecution. We, as intercessors will share in His persecution more than most. Let's just be real, an intercessor is hated by both church people as well as by the world. I also discovered that I don't particularly enjoy the tests and trials, but if that is the only way to attain the necessary knowledge, strength, and wisdom to do the will of God then so be it. And if God will be with us, as we have discovered that He is always with us, we can go through whatever He allows in order for us to grow and go to another level. Hopefully, this is what we're all saying. But the way I see it, there is really no other choice if we are going to be used by God to reach souls.

We have been called for such a time as this and must do something significant for the kingdom of God. The Lord Jesus Christ gave us all power and all authority over all power of the enemy. In order for us to walk in that power and authority, we have to abide in the Lord Jesus Christ and let the Word of God abide in us. The Lord Jesus also stated in John 15:7 that we cannot do anything on our own except fail, and only when we are connected to Him can we succeed. He further stated that if we abide in Him, and He in us, we can bear fruit or be of use to the kingdom of God. Just as the branch cannot bear fruit of itself except it abide in the vine, so we cannot bear fruit except we abide in the Lord Jesus Christ. As a result, we, saints have to be very careful as to what we allow ourselves to meditate on. This includes what we watch, what we listen to, and what we talk about. When we allow ungodly, worldly things to occupy our thoughts, we become what we think. We also become hardened and callous to the things of God. This will, in turn, bring about confusion, and will cause us to be unable to hear the voice of God, and will lead us to lean to our on understanding. When we find ourselves making decisions and performing actions without consulting, God, we have stepped outside of the protection and direction of God. This is when people begin to make evil and sinful decisions that seem to be right to us at the time, but leads to death and destruction in the long run. This means that we are being deceived by the enemy who attacks us thorough our own minds.

When we are under attack of the enemy, we are completely unable to focus and delve into the Word of God or totally surrender to the things of God. Although, the enemy might succeed in taking us off course for a time, there is always a way back. God, himself, has provided a way to get refocused, to get our hearing sharpened, and to return to exercising Godly wisdom in all of our decisions. The way back is through the written and spoken Word of God. This is the only way to totally obliterate the ungodly thoughts and eradicate the evil actions. The Word of God can so clean our spirits from the dirtiness of the world just as soap can cleanse dirt off of us in the natural. The Word of God is the only way to get back to seeing, hearing, and thinking wisely. I have also observed that the average Christian or intercessor is not allowing their characters to be developed and their fruit to be cultivated. In other words, we, Christians can be filled overflowing with the Holy Spirit of GOD and still be bankrupt in their characters; thereby, producing corrupt fruit, unproductive fruit or even rotten fruit—hence the saying, so heavenly minded, but no earthly good or so earthly minded and no spiritually good. Because an intercessor is very sensitive in the spirit and have been entrusted with the gift of the spirit of discernment, we have to be very, very careful of whatever comes our way by looking longer and digging deeper and praying harder in order to operate accurately in God's precious and powerful gifts.

Chapter Ten

CHARACTER DEVELOPMENT IN THE BODY OF CHRIST

"But the fruit of the Spirit is love, joy, peace, longsuffering, gentleness, goodness, faith, meekness, temperance; Against such there is no law." Galatians 5:22–23

THE ULTIMATE GOAL of every born again Christian is to possess, manifest, and display the characteristics of the Lord Jesus Christ in our lives. This is a process that entails a willing and obedient mind, will, and spirit and requires total yielding to the Holy Spirit. We have to be prepared to allow God to take us down the path He chooses and orchestrate our steps as He deems fit in order to reach the desired result of fulfilling our God-given purposes in the earth. In order to allow character development or fruit production, we must have an intimate relationship with the Lord, where we are connected mind to mind and heart to heart with Him. A lot of saints express genuine surprise that we can have such an on-going, intimate relationship with the Lord. This kind of intimate relationship can be developed over time only if we are willing to pursue it. In doing so, this will be some of the times in our Christian walk that will be the most painful and the most uncomfortable. The pain will come due to our having to tell our flesh no and God yes. As we know, this is something that people are not accustomed to doing for very long. Although, we love the Lord and long to please Him, our character development is an on-going process, and it seems that we're always taking tests in the kingdom, so to speak. I believe this processing and growing will continue until we leave the earth.

Some of the most important components needed for character development that appear to be missing from a large majority of saints today are tenacity, consistency, genuine care and love for others, and a forgiving spirit. A tenacious persevering spirit is so very important, and is a missing component from a lot of our characters. It is of the utmost importance because if we don't stay in the fight, we will automatically lose. In order to be used, all intercessors must have that staying power. Another important character component is faith. First of all, intercessors have to be pleasing to God, and having faith in GOD is the way to be pleasing to God. The scripture reads, "But without faith, it is impossible to please Him". Heb.11:6. Then, the character component of consistency is just as important because God, your sisters, your brothers in Christ as well as others in every area of our lives must be able testify that we are people that keep our word. Because we are representatives of the living God in the earth, it is so very urgent that we can be depended upon. As a reflection of the God we serve, we are to be consistent as the world is desperately looking for consistency from the body of Christ. The character component of love for God and for your fellow man is by far the most important to an intercessor's character development. This component is so important to Jesus that He left as His final commandment His desire for us to have love for one another and to show this love to one another. I believe one of the reasons He commanded us to have love one to the other is because

God is love. He went on to say that, we, as saints of God will be identified by the world by our love to one another. The scripture reads, "A new commandment I give unto you that ye love one another as I have loved you, that ye also love one another," John 13:34. Therefore, walking in love is walking in obedience to God. The scripture reads, "If ye love me, keep my commandments." John 14:15. When operating in this commandment of God then and only then, will we be able to intercede for others--not only in our own church, our own city, our own house, but in other cities, states, and nations. In other words, God will use us right from our own prayer closet/room to intercede for someone on the other side of the world! The Bible goes on to teach us in the book of 1 Corinthians 13 that if we don't have love, we are tantamount to a resounding gong or a clanging cymbal and is nothing nor will gain anything. But with love, we will never fail.

Just as there are some character components to go after, there are also some components to stay away from. Components such as evil thoughts, a prideful stance, and a lying tongue, just to name a few. We must be very careful of our thoughts—even those so called good thoughts. For example, when God uses us and our thoughts are constantly on that incident or occasion instead of on God, then pride is trying to take over or attach itself to us. This will stop God's presence every time. The closer we get to God, the higher we will go in the Spirit, and the easier it will be for us to die to ourselves and our self-interests. We must learn to read our own spiritual markers. We cannot depend upon man's opinion, no matter who it is, whether it is your Pastor, parents, spouse, etc. not saying to dishonor or disrespect anyone, but we must not depend upon any flesh more than we depend upon our Father God, the Lord Jesus, and the Holy Spirit.

We are required to be so full of the love of God that we are naturally over flowing with it, so much so, that it spills over onto whomever comes across our path or vice versa. To reiterate, our Lord's last commandment to us was a commandment to be toward each other as He is toward us. He said that this would be the way that we would be identified as His followers because of our infectious, genuine love for one another. This commandment has not been widely practiced in the Christian community, as of late, at least not as much as it should be. I really believe the lack of genuine love is a very significant reason that the body of Christ is being succumbed to the same types of traps of the enemy that the world has succumbed.

Character development is deficient in the body of Christ as we, the saints of God, do not keep ourselves consecrated, purified and holy enough to walk in the authority Jesus gave us. There is no fear of the enemy when we know that we are clean—consecrated, purified, and holy. When we have totally surrendered ourselves to the Lord, we can walk in that boldness the apostles walked in and in the authority the apostles walked in. We must decrease so Jesus can increase. Just as John had to purposely step down and put himself in subjection to the Lord, so must we abase ourselves and yield to the leading of the Holy Spirit and let go of the things of the world so that Jesus can be lifted up. We are thankful that the Lord does not require our actual physical deaths but only our spiritual deaths to self. For the Christian, there is no separation of how we live whether at church, at home, at work, or even at play. This involves our business practices as well as our political affiliations. Being a Christian is who we are and not what we do. We are to be people of integrity and invoke the Word and commandments of God into whatever or wherever our daily lives lead us. God will not put more on us than we can bear. We are to never, ever lean to our own understanding or rely on and be led by emotional attachments. Remember, God is intently watching over every area of our lives. As we grow spiritually and go to a higher level in God, the Lord God equips us to combat the stronger attacks of the enemy. In other words, before the stronger attacks come, God has already equipped us to resist them and walk in authority over them. God cannot and will not leave us defenseless against the enemy.

In addition to lack of certain character component development, some very noticeable changes that have taken place within our churches. In fact, some things have drastically changed in our churches. One of the first and most prevalent changes that have taken place is that there is a lack of generosity. The kind of generosity that was very evident in the early Christian church that is depicted in the book of Acts, Chapter 4:34–35. The love of God was so much a part of the lives of the early saints, that they had no qualms about selling properties and sharing with the rest of the saints that were in need. Today, we see very little of this kind of love and care for others in the body of Christ. Actually, it has gotten very difficult to get the saints of God to consistently pay tithe. As an intercessor, we have to know that Jesus does not enter into casual relationships. He will only enter into covenant relationships. I have observed that a lot of intercessors and saints are trying to have a relationship with both the Lord and the world, simultaneously. When we are born again, we should no longer be occupied by time because we are eternal beings that are confident that what we do for the kingdom of GOD will last forever, and will follow us to heaven.

Chapter Eleven

CARING FOR THE TEMPLE

"What? Know ye not that your body is the temple of the Holy Ghost which is in you, which ye have of God, and ye are not your own?" 1 Corinthians 6:19.

J CAN SAY WITHOUT hesitation that there are very few of us saints caring for our temples as we're commanded to do in the Word of God. Although, I make this statement very cautiously, after careful observation, I have to be honest and say that it appears that the body of Christ are some of the most obese and sickly people on the face of this earth. Now, let me begin by putting myself on the list of falling down on the job when it comes to the taking good care of my temple as I should. I must confess that I am just as guilty of eating the wrong things and eating too much of the wrong things much too often. Yes, I am in a battle to take authority over my very strong, thriving appetite for the wrong foods! Believe you me, I will be the first to tell you just how difficult it is to develop and maintain healthy eating habits. I will also tell you that the excessive eating is not just a lack of discipline, but it is also the result of attacks from the enemy. I know it sounds as if I'm trying to pass the blame, and I realize that we have the ultimate responsibility when it comes to taking care of God's temples. But, what I want everyone to realize is that there is an enemy who has come to steal, kill, and destroy, and he does not care how he accomplishes his mission. He is not above setting up scenarios to tempt us and lie to us as he did to Eve in Garden of Eden. Let me assure you, he is still trying to cause us to fail today. In order to take control of our bodies as we should, we have to know exactly what we're up against and how to defeat it. Only then will we be able to accurately approach the issue of caring for our temples, and be able to accurately discern how to take authority in all areas of our temples. First of all, we are not realizing that the proper care for our temples are a multifaceted duty. Additionally, this is a duty that has to be taken more seriously by the body of Christ in order to successfully complete our work in the earth. The proper upkeep of our temples is multifaceted because it involves our spirits, souls, and bodies. This awesome responsibility that has been afforded to us to take care of our temples require the protecting and the feeding of our spirits, souls, and bodies in equal increments. Somehow, the body of Christ have been duped into believing that the spiritual segment of our temple upkeep responsibility is more important than the others. Yes, we can go through life with a minimal amount of functioning if we continue to neglect one or the other, but we will not ever experience the maximum potential that is possible with the total temple care and upkeep package. For years, we have been shocked and even mortified when we hear of the untimely passing of a man or woman of God. Granted, not all of them were in bad health or obese, but a large number of them were in failing health. It appears that the church has taken no consideration of what we are putting in our bodies until we are under a doctor's care. From the very beginning, God has put great importance on what we put in our mouths and in our ears. In the Old Testament, God took the time to dictate to Moses exactly what He required the children of Israel to eat and not to eat. He even sent them food directly from heaven with instruction. The scripture reads, "This is the thing which the LORD hath commanded, Gather of it every man according to his eating, an omer for every man, according to the number of your persons; take ye every man for them which are in his tents." Exodus 16:16. God also constantly warned the children of Israel concerning their associations in both marriage and business. In other words, He wanted them to stay away from anyone or anything that would influence them to stray away from Him. Granted, most of the body of Christ are well aware of the spiritual segment, and they do put forth a certain amount of effort into paying attention to that aspect more by attending church, paying tithe, and reading some scripture. We are even receiving more teaching about and are accepting that there must be a renewing of our minds as the scripture teaches. We are also being taught how to take control over all of our soulish realm (mind, will, and emotions) by learning to speak what we want and are also making some progress in growing our faith in that arena.

Regretfully, an alarming number of the body of Christ are completely neglecting our physical bodies in the caring for our temples as we are commanded in the scripture. Our physical bodies which is a part of the overall requirement for temple maintenance is just as important as the other aspects of caring for our temples. In some cases, our bodies, in the body of Christ, are being both neglected and abused. In order to be successful in fulfilling our destinies, we must have all aspects of our temple upkeep clicking on all cylinders. In other words, we must be aware of every area for service in the kingdom of God. As we're taught in the scripture, our bodies are the temples of the Holy Spirit. Because this aspect of caring for the temple is the most neglected, we are not and cannot receive everything that God so desperately wants to impart into us. In order to do the work that has to be done for such a time as this, we must begin to work on this area. So many of the saints of God, simply, do not have the stamina it takes to carry the anointing that is needed to operate in the authority that has been designated to us from the Lord. We are all so sickly and so tired that we can barely go from our cars to the church pews, let alone, pray as we should for other people. Heaven forbid that we're ever asked to cast out a demon or ever have to pray for someone's deliverance. This kind of kingdom work can sometimes require much more time than does a regular prayer. It might even require an extended or overnight prayer session. How many of the body of Christ are prepared to pray all night if need be? Of course, we might desire to obey the Lord and try and do what is needed, but our own bodies will prevent us because of a lack of strength or because of a sickness. We certainly will not have the stamina and strength to carry the anointing for any period of time if we do not take better care of ourselves because the anointing and the presence of the Holy Spirit is heavy— literally. The realization that taking care of our physical bodies is as important as taking care of our spirits and souls is something that the enemy wants to keep us in the dark concerning. He wants to keep the scales upon our eyes and keep the importance of being in good physical shape to carry the anointing hidden from the saints of God. We can look around in the church and observe that the enemy's strategy is working very well from his standpoint. Unfortunately, a very large number of the saints of God are very sickly as we speak. He loves it when the body of Christ are just as sickly as the world. He wants us to believe that the conditions of our physical, spiritual, and soul realms are totally separate from one another. He really wants us to totally neglect our physical bodies by shunning all form of exercise, by eating unhealthy, and by continually overeating and overstressing. The enemy does not want us to know that by neglecting the upkeep of our physical bodies, we are in disobedience to the scripture that tells us not to defile the temple of God. The scripture reads, "Know ye not that ye are the temple of God and that the Spirit of God dwelleth in you? If any man defiles the temple of God, him shall God destroy; for the temple of God is holy, which temple ye are." 1 Corinthians 3:1616–17. Clearly, the Lord requires us to care for our temples. If we think about it, we must become aware of and be vigilant concerning every area that the enemy can possibly try and use to hinder God's work in the earth. Regardless of our current physical conditions, whether good or bad, we all need to continually improve in that area. We already know we need to continually improve in our spiritual and soulish realms. As with everything concerning our lives, we must seek God's divine help. We must ask Him for guidance in the upkeep of every aspect of caring for our temples in order to complete our individual assignments. I believe the scripture tells us in the Book of 3 John that every area of our lives should be prospering at the same rate or the same time. The scripture reads, "Beloved, I wish above all things that thou mayest prosper and be in health, even as thy soul prospereth." 3 John 1:2. Ultimately, we know that if we're not feeling well or if we're always tired and have no energy, we are very limited in what we can accomplish for the kingdom of God, whether spiritual or physical. Finally, if we are not at our best, we cannot receive God's best; therefore, we cannot give out the best which is what is needed to represent and build the kingdom of God.

Chapter Twelve

LET HIM KILL YOU

"And he said to them all, if any man will come after me, let him deny himself, and take up his cross daily, and follow me." Luke 9:23

"And whosoever doth not bear his cross, and come after me, cannot be my disciple." Luke 14:27

THE MOST IMPORTANT but least discussed requirement for the ministry of intercession is death—ours. No, not our physical deaths, but death to our flesh (mind, will, emotions). God is desperately searching for saints that are willing to die. Saints that are willing to let Him have His way in them in order to accomplish His plans for us to take our rightful places in authority over the enemy. He also wants to use us to bring souls into the kingdom. Unfortunately, we do not readily access our spiritual lives from the standpoint of life and death as we should. Although, it is highly unusual to approach our service to the kingdom of God from this positive or negative perspective, I believe it is very beneficial to do so because a lot of the saints of God are under the misnomer that once we become born again, all negative aspects of our lives should and will cease. We, really, believe we will not be tested. In actuality, our entire lives are a test. Everything we do, say, and think is being evaluated by God. I'm not saying we have to walk around on eggshells thinking that God is out to get us. What I am saying is, God is searching for someone He can trust with His heart. Someone He can trust to obey His word. If we are to do anything meaningful for the kingdom of God, we are going to have to let Him teach us in His own way. This is especially true for the intercessor, the prayer warriors. We have to be willing to let God take over and be willing to lay our lives down and take up our crosses and follow Jesus. We have to trust the Lord to lead us even when the way He's taking us seem to be too treacherous, too harsh, and/or too frightening. We have to trust that His Word is true, and that He will take us through to the other side to a better place. Remember, unlike the worldly system, the way of God, and the path up to victory in His kingdom is down. No, not down and forgotten, but down in the care and protection of almighty God until He deems us ready for the task at hand. This is when and where, we, the children of God will receive strength, wisdom, power, and love. These are the pertinent qualities that are required for the saint of God to always be in charge and attain victory and reign supreme in the face of all of life's various circumstances and attacks of the enemy.

As we look at some of the negative aspects of being an intercessor such as great persecution, loneliness, being misunderstood, being ostracized, etc., we are encouraged when we take the time to look at the other side—the positive. When we allow God, He will open our eyes to the positives of salvation, healing, deliverance, protection, etc. that far, far outweigh any negatives. In order for intercessors to succeed in spite of the negative aspects, we must know how to speak things into manifestation. In order to speak things into the seen realm from the unseen realm, we must have faith. We must have faith in God, believing that He is and that

He is a rewarder of them who diligently seek Him. We must have faith, believing what we say shall come to pass and not doubting in your hearts. Hebrews 11:6. In order to successfully walk in this kind of faith and accomplish the mandate to bring in the great end time harvest that we have been put into the earth for at this time, we must let God do a work in us. A killing work. Most of us are more than willing to be a part of the work of God, but we're not as willing to let God get us prepared for that work. If we do not let God get us prepared, we will be forever fighting the wrong battles and getting very badly beaten. We must come to the understanding that there are a lot of battles being waged, but the participants are not only fighting the wrong battles but the wrong enemy. For ages, the enemy has successfully diverted the attention of the body of Christ into focusing on the wrong thing while he is steadily spreading confusion and destruction. It is written, "Satan is the father of lies." John 8:44. This means that lying originated with the enemy. It also means that the very first lie to come into the earth realm came in by the enemy. Genesis, Chapter 3.

An intercessor must recognize the anointing, be anointed, and operate in the anointing which can only come by some flesh crushing and some dying to self. The anointing on a person is a deterrent to the negativity that the enemy tries to inject. The anointing is a positive because people see the beauty of JESUS on us when we're operating under the anointing of God. When we spend time in prayer and the presence of God, we don't have to ever doubt if our prayers will be answered. There should not be any doubt even when we don't immediately see the results of our prayers or petitions to God. The level of the anointing that we must walk in as the body of Christ can only be downloaded into us by the very presence of God. Contrary to popular belief that everyone who's been called to the ministry are anointed, the yoke breaking anointing can only come via death to self under the direction of the Lord. God says in His Word that He is nigh unto those of a broken heart and a contrite spirit. If we stay the course and let God complete the work that He has started in us, we can be ready for God to use us for such a time as this. When He is done in us, we will come forth as pure gold. Sadly, the majority of the saints are having great difficulty in being consistent and are fluctuating between what they really believe, especially, when things begin to get a little difficult.

The scripture goes on to tell us that the trying of our faith worketh patience. "My brethren, count it all joy when ye fall into divers temptations; Knowing this, that the trying of your faith worketh patience. But let patience have her perfect work, that ye may be perfect and entire, wanting nothing." James 1: 2–4.

A dead saint will stand for God in the face of some, seemingly, insurmountable odds. A dead saint will never try and get revenge. As a dead saint, we realize that we are no longer our own, but our bodies are the temples of the Holy Spirit. We cannot get to or succeed in the ministry of intercession, living. It is an absolute must that we die to self, and we must crush the flesh. Only a dead "man" can truly intercede. We, as the body of Christ, have spurts of dying; but there are very few of us who are consistently dead. As an intercessor, in addition to dying to self, we must be careful to die to the accolades of man. We must be very mindful of caring about and getting caught up in the latest trick of the devil concerning how many people like and/or follow us. This trick is designed to cause us to compromise our long held beliefs just to have a certain number of likes or followers. The enemy is trying to cause us to have a fixation on self which is rooted in the spirit of pride. There is nothing that will cause the flesh to rise up in domination to try stay alive more than the spirit of pride. As we know, this spirit is one of the things that God explicitly hates. The scripture reads, "These six things doth the LORD hate; yea, seven are an abomination unto him. A proud look, a lying tongue, and hands that shed innocent blood ..." Proverbs 6:1–17. The kingdom of God is filled to the brim with saints that refuse to die. I believe that is why God is saying that the harvest is plenteous, but the laborers are few. How can God use us when we're always focused on ourselves and are often as offended and angry as the world we're trying to win? The Lord says, if we try and save our lives, we will lose it. The scripture reads, "For whosoever will save his life shall lose it, but whosoever shall lose his life for my sake and the gospel's the same shall save it." Mark 8:35. We must allow God to kill us totally by submitting ourselves to His will for our lives. Wanted: saints that are willing to die in order to stay alive and bring in the harvest!

Chapter Thirteen

STAYING DEAD -
MATURE SAINTS

"Whom shall he teach knowledge? And whom shall he make to understand doctrine? Them that are weaned from the milk, and drawn from the breasts." Isaiah 28:9

I N ORDER FOR us to remain yielded and submitted to God and stay dead to the things of the flesh as is required for the call to the ministry of intercession, we have to do as Paul and reckon ourselves dead to sin and alive to God through Christ Jesus. The scripture reads, "Likewise reckon ye also yourselves to be dead indeed unto sin, but alive unto God through Jesus Christ our Lord." Romans 6:11. God is looking for someone who will immediately run to Him in the name of Jesus when we encounter the things that are causing our flesh to come alive. He is seeking mature saints who know how to critique themselves before they look outward at others. This takes a level of maturity that is very rare in this "me" generation. This level of maturity can only be accomplished by praying, Bible studying saints—no other way! To put it bluntly, in the spirit, the flesh has to be killed on a continual basis. Only a regular regimen of the Word and the presence of God can do it. God expects His children to grow up in the Spirit just as children are expected to grow up in the natural. In maturing, we have to constantly bring our body (flesh) under subjection. The scripture teaches, "But I keep under my body, and bring it into subjection; lest that by any means, when I have preached to others, I myself should be a castaway." 1 Corinthians 9:27. You see, our flesh (mind, body, will, and emotions) are our enemies. They will constantly align themselves with the enemy of our souls, the devil. As a mature saint, we must readily recognize who the enemies are, and speedily bring those enemies down. The scripture teaches us to bring every thought captive to the obedience of God. The scripture reads, "Casting down imaginations, and every high thing that exalteth itself against the knowledge of God, and bringing into captivity every thought to the obedience of Christ." 2 Corinthians 10:5. This means that it all begins with our thought lives which affects our emotional lives and in turn our actions. If we do not bring our thoughts captive and always lean to our own understanding, we are setting ourselves up for failure because as I stated earlier, we cannot trust our own mind, will, and emotions. They are constantly waiting for the opportunity to betray us. You see, at any given time, any one of us can be overcome by an emotion or thought that is so strong and so pervasive that we believe that it must be right and from God. Sadly, to say, the vast majority of supposedly mature saints live their lives this way. We feel that we do not need to pray and fast on it because it is so overwhelming so it has to be God. Wrong! It is God only if it is in the Word of God. God will never, ever speak anything to us that is contrary to His written Word! Mature and dead saints know this!

As we study and feed on the Word of God, God expects us to grow thereby. For instance, when a child is born, it is expected to grow physically, mentally, and emotionally according to the standards and criteria that have been set in place by the experts. If the child fails to progress or grow in these areas, it becomes apparent that there is something very wrong and the child needs special help. Usually, the child will be tested in various areas and in various ways to determine what is the problem. In the meantime, there will be certain tasks and/or responsibilities that will be withheld from the child. Likewise, if we do not grow up in the Spirit, and if we do not begin to eat meat, but are always feeding on milk, we will be limited as to how God can use us. For instance, if we, as saints, are still bickering over denominations and are not walking in love or are not exhibiting the fruit of the Spirit and are still being offended and refusing correction, and are not taking authority over the enemy with our health situations, while the enemy is taking people out, we are not going to be used of God as we desire. God is waiting and looking for some grown-up saints with the likes of Moses and Paul that He can trust to have His heart and have the mind of Christ. God is looking for some people that He can trust to make some heavenly, righteous executive decisions in the earth without taking advantage of God and God's people. Someone who is dead to the flesh and alive in the Spirit of God. God so trusted Moses and Paul in the Spirit that He allowed or gave them the freedom make some critical decisions and to give their opinions concerning some critical life situations. For instance, God allowed Moses to write a bill of divorcement John 8 and Paul to give his opinion on marriage 1 Corinthians 7.

I'm learning that there a large number of born again believers in Jesus that still desire to follow the crowd. They want to lean toward who or what is most popular. This is, especially, evident in our current political culture. Alarmingly, there are a lot of seasoned saints, seemingly, confused concerning their stance in the political arena. The fact that a born again Christian has to question where they stand is a very obvious sign that something is systemically wrong in the body of Christ. The kind of mature saint that God is looking for in these very troubled times would not have to hesitate for a second, but they immediately know and attest that if a certain political agenda is going against God's Word, it is also going against their beliefs. This also highlights the fact that the body of Christ is carrying around some generational baggage that must be thrown out or obliterated. In addition, this also exposes the fact that we, the church, have to become much more serious concerning the renewing of our minds. As we know, only the Word of God can renew our minds. We cannot be casual acquaintances with the Word, but we must serious students of God's Word in order to survive in today's culture. This survival encompasses the spiritual and the natural aspects of our lives and the lives of our families. The enemy will always confront us with things or circumstances that seem to be right in our own eyes, but it is wrong in the eyes of God. Only the Word of God can expertly shine the light on every trick or trap of the enemy. These are what the Bible refers to as the "small foxes", and they play a very significant role in holding us back from receiving God's best. Mature saints that are serious Bible students and pray warriors will be more prepared to recognize these, seemingly, insignificant things that are so craftily perpetuated by the enemy. Mature saints do not walk around with offense in their hearts while refusing to reconcile with their brother and sister in Christ. They do not neglect to pay their tithes and offerings. Mature saints are dependable and always punctual. God is looking for saints that He doesn't have to correct every minute of every day. God is looking for saints that believe His word, and are not constantly murmuring and questioning His commandments. While, we, the saints of God are wasting precious time asking God why we have not seen the promises He made come to pass, we should be looking within ourselves as to why we have not seen the promises come to fruition. We should be asking what must we do or rather what have we left undone. If we are honest, we all can attest to the fact that we have some issues that still have to be confronted and eradicated. He is looking for saints that will stand on the Word and are not being swayed by every evil trick of the devil. God is looking for saints that are mature to the point of total submission and obedience. Maturing and staying dead to self is an on-going position of the intercessor and saint of God. We must always keep this stance in order to be able to declare as did Jesus when He stated that the enemy had nothing in Him. It is written in the scripture as follows: "Hereafter I will not talk much with you; for the prince of this world cometh, and hath nothing in me." John 14:30. We can attain this status in the Spirit if we constantly stay on guard checking our hearts, our actions, and our motivations for everything we do. The scripture teaches us that if we do this ourselves, we will not have to be taken to task by the Spirit of God for our actions later. The scripture reads, "For if we would judge ourselves, we should not be judged. But when we are judged, we are chastened of the Lord, that we should not be condemned with the world." 1 Corinthians 11:31. A mature saint is a dead saint that continually dies!

Chapter Fourteen

CONSECRATION

"For the law maketh men high priests which have infirmity;
but the word of the oath which was since the law, maketh
the Son, who is consecrated for evermore." Hebrews 7:28

W E AS INTERCESSORS are supposed to live a life of consecration, separation, holiness, and purification in order to always be in the position for God to use us effectively. When we are called to the ministry of intercession, we are also being called to be consecrated. This consecration has been made available to us by accepting the Lord Jesus Christ as our savior believing that we are sanctified through the offering of His body once and for all, and believing that His shed blood at Calvary washed away our sins. We must be consecrated and separated unto God with our eyes, with our associates, with our words, with what is going into our ears, with what comes out of our mouths, with our thoughts, and with our actions and especially with our reactions. Being consecrated and set aside for God's use in today's society dictates that we must be very careful of our associations and with whom we align ourselves spiritually, physically, and politically. It all matters to God more than we realize. Only in and by the shed blood of Jesus do we have boldness to enter into the Holy of Holies and by which we have been given a new and living way, which He has consecrated for us, through the His own flesh. The scripture reads, "By a new and living way, which he hath consecrated for us, through the veil, that is to say, his flesh;" Hebrews 10:20.

In order for the Lord to call us apart and do a work in us to even get us in a position to be consecrated unto Himself as an intercessor, we must have pure hearts, clean hands, and sincere motivations. An intercessor must be trustworthy in the spiritual and in the natural; we must not only be someone that God can trust with His heart, but we must be able to be trusted in our homes, on our jobs, and with our neighbors. In order to survive, an intercessor must abide under the shadow of the Almighty at all times. As an intercessor, sometimes it's just good to be with or spend time with the Lord without saying anything—just communing with Him spirit to Spirit as He knows the heart of everyone. For example, when two people, a man and a woman are dating, there are times they will be together and not say an audible word to each other, yet, they have spoken volumes to each other just by being in each other's presence. That is the same way it is, sometimes, when we spend quality time with God. It is just good to be with the Lord God, the Lord Jesus, the Holy Spirit. These qualities and this stance is what, we, as an intercessor and even the body of Christ should fight for with all of our might each and every day. There are no shortcuts to getting in the presence of God and to walking in the anointing of God.

Because an intercessor is a direct and major threat to the enemy, it is imperative for an intercessor to stay very close to God at all times. We must always stay in close proximity to the Lord in order to hear His directions on every aspect of our lives at all times. This includes our friendships, our entertainment, our jobs, and even our shopping—everything. Because the garments and/

or lifestyle of an intercessor is unique, there are some activities that might not be a sin, but will be forbidden to us as intercessors by the Holy Spirit—sometimes temporarily and sometimes permanently.

We must not take God's anointing and prostitute it by using it in our own way. It is very dangerous to take God's anointing and not cultivate the fruit of the Holy Spirit. The scripture reads, "But the fruit of the Spirit is love, joy, peace, longsuffering, gentleness, goodness, faith, meekness, temperance; against such there is no law." Gal. 5:22. It is possible to preach, or do the work of God and miss the will of God ourselves. The scripture reads, "Not everyone that saith unto me, Lord, Lord, shall enter into the kingdom of heaven, but he that doeth the will of my Father which is in heaven…And then will I profess unto them, I never knew you: depart from me, ye that work iniquity. Matt.7:21–24. It is not what is the outer covering of a person that makes a person who they are, but what is within. The outside, which can be seen with the naked eye, is not the person. What we can see is merely the covering for the actual person. There are things that God will not show to intercessors that are not consecrated as required. We have to be in that place of consecration for the explicit reason to receive what to speak or pray into the earth realm. For instance, there were two people that God had shown that Jesus, the Messiah, would come into the earth because, I believe, they were intercessors used by God to pray this prophecy into being as we will further explore in another area of *Commanding the Forces*. These two people are Anna, the prophetess and Simeon, a spirit-filled, just, and devout man of Jerusalem. Luke 2:25–39.

To maintain the qualifications to be set apart as a consecrated intercessor, we must be tenacious, determined and steadfast in our prayer lives. Most importantly, an intercessor must have a pure heart, clean hands, pure motivations and be obedient to God, totally. An intercessor must know how to take authority in the spiritual realm and how to walk in faith.

Fasting is an integral part of a consecrated intercessor's life. In order for an intercessor to walk in constant authority over the enemy and to remain spiritually strengthened, they must fast consistently. This is not an option but a necessity in being consecrated unto the Lord. The Holy Spirit will also lead us on fasts. There are some spiritual battles that can only be won with prayer and fasting. The scripture reads, "And when he was come into the house his disciples asked him privately, Why could not we cast him out? And he said unto them, This kind can come forth by nothing, but by prayer and fasting." Mark 9:28–29.

An effective, called aside, set apart for the use of God saint must be in a constant renewing of their minds in the Word of God. A consecrated intercessor has to live their lives totally and completely purified by being washed in the Word. We must stay in a place where we can be corrected by the Holy Spirit. It is almost like the priest of the Old Testament that would go into the Holy of Holies to offer sacrifice on behalf of the people. He had to be sure that he was clean or else he would not come out alive. An intercessor will be tested in every area--I should say thoroughly tested in every area.

In allowing God to consecrate us, we must be content to stay in the background and watch as our prayers are answered, giving glory to God always, without letting our flesh rise up. In the kingdom of God, lesser is greater. The behind the scene ministry is always the most powerful. This is not a ministry for the faint hearted. This ministry requires us to be quiet even when everything in us longs to speak. As a consecrated intercessor, we will be called to pray for people that do not, and in some cases will never know we are praying for them on this earth. Only as a consecrated intercessor can we be trusted to pray for the people that treat us the worst and hate us the most. As a consecrated intercessor, we cannot ever discuss some of our prayer assignments from God, especially with the one we're praying for.

Consecrated intercessors are to be carriers of the presence of the living God. Whenever or wherever we show up, there should be a shifting in the atmosphere. Our very presence should be so weighty because of the anointing that we carry that there is a change in whatever place we visit no matter the capacity. Because of the weight of our spirits, we should be missed when we are not in a particular place, just as our presence is felt when we are in a particular place. This weight can only be obtained by spending time with the Lord Jesus Christ. Intercession is not what you do but who you are. For example, an intercessor is not just Bob the intercessor, but is Bob intercessor just as Jesus is called Jesus Christ, Christ is not His last name but who He is. So it should be with an intercessor.

The more you know God, the more you have to know the Word of God, and the greater your revelations from God, the more danger you're in spiritually--with both heaven and hell. With heaven because the more you know, the more accountable you are. The scripture reads, "For unto whomsoever much is given, of him shall be much required; and to whom men have committed much, of him they will ask the more." Luke 12:48. With hell because you become even more hated by the enemy who desires to stop you at any cost. The scripture reads, "The thief cometh not, but for to steal, and to kill, and to destroy; I am come that they might have life and that they might have it more abundantly." John 10:10. Let's stay under the umbrella of God's protection by staying consecrated by God.

Chapter Fifteen

INTERCESSORY GARMENT REQUIREMENTS

"But when the king came in to view the guests, he looked intently at a man there who had on no wedding garment. And he said, Friend, how did you come in here without putting on the [appropriate] wedding garment? And he was speechless (muzzled, gagged)." Matthew 11–12 AMP

A S WE PROGRESS in our relationship with God, we quickly learn that God's ways are higher than our ways, and His thoughts are higher than our thoughts as the scripture teaches. We also come to the realization that there are commandments and mandates that God has set forth for us to follow without any deviation. As intercessors, we find that there is an order by which we have to yield to in order to receive anything from God. I believe one of the mandates of God is that we must be properly dressed in the required attire of heaven. What are the garments of a properly dressed intercessor? The scripture reads, "To appoint unto them that mourn in Zion, to give unto them beauty for ashes the oil of joy for mourning, the garment of praise for the spirit of heaviness that they might be called trees of righteousness, the planting of the LORD, that He might be glorified." Isaiah 61:3 The proper dress—either in the spirit or in the natural world—require a different approach for an intercessor before the Lord. For example, in the natural world, there is one way I can be dressed in my bedroom, but there is another way I have to be dressed in the prayer room on the threshing floor. The very approach is totally different.

The intercessor and the body of Christ must be dressed in the Spirit of Christ. To begin, we must possess and cannot survive without this garment. Some of the other required garments for properly dressed intercessors are: we must know who is the enemy, we must develop patience, we must be people of integrity, we must be free of offenses, we must be quick to forgive, we must be steadfast and persevere, and we must live a fasted lifestyle. We are required to pursue and to possess them. As intercessors, we must know that this is how we're to be dressed every day. This is our lifestyle, and not something that we do occasionally. Prayer and the Word of God is our nourishment and our lifeline. We must feed off of them every day in order to stay strong in the Spirit because the enemy watches us for any sign of weakness. If we are not properly fed every day, this will make us weak which will only cause us to become more susceptible to his attacks. The weaker we are spiritually, the more our flesh will dictate to us, but the stronger we become spiritually, the more we will dictate to the flesh. We will be able to bring the flesh under subjection. As we already know, God, our Father, requires certain things to be done in a certain way. Some additional garment requirements are: We must walk in obedience, we must seek God with all of our hearts, with all of our minds, and with all of our souls. We must be trustworthy to God and to ourselves, and in all aspects, we must be trustworthy both spiritually and naturally. Each time we put on one or more of the garments, they will be tested to see if they are "fitting" properly. Some of the required fruit and/or attributes that will be manifested when properly clothed in the spiritual garments of an intercessor are *love, faith, and integrity.*

Although, we have touched on having the love of God in other chapters of *Commanding the Forces,* it is such an important fruit that it is worth taking a little closer look. There is no reason not to love if we belong to JESUS, and if we are filled with His Spirit. Because God is love and lives in us, we have the capacity to walk in the commandment that JESUS gave to us, to love one to another. The scripture reads, "This is my commandment, that ye love one another, as I have loved you. Greater love hath no man than this, that a man lay down his life for his friends. Ye are my friends, if ye do whatsoever I command you." John 15:12–14. To love is a direct commandment from God and is not just a suggestion. Although, as Christians, we have been endowed with that love, to operate in that love is still a choice. In order to love as God has commanded us to do is not ever dependent upon any outward manifestation from the recipients of our love. God is love and if God resides on the inside of us—in our hearts, then we have the required love. Walking in that love, and living the love life is the only true indication that we are truly children of God and belong to the Lord Jesus Christ. The scripture reads, "A new commandment I give unto you, That ye love one another, as I have loved you, that ye also love one another." John 13:34

As Paul writes in 1 Corinthians 13, If you don't have love, then you don't have anything. Our ability to withstand and persevere in love is a sure sign that you are an intercessor. An intercessor will sustain a multitude of attacks from whomever the devil can use. When we are able to stand and still love in spite is how we'll know whether or not we're called to the ministry of intercession. It is how we'll know that we are someone on whom God can depend. The attacks are and will always be on-going. There will be times when we are hated by almost everyone even on the inside of the church due to the calling that is on our lives. We are expected to reciprocate in love only. We are called to share in the fellowship of His suffering. This entails being able to feel His pain and the grieving of the Holy Spirit, and to understand the Father's heart in loving those that do not, readily, return that love. Perfect love casteth out all fear. The scripture reads, "There is no fear in love, but perfect love casteth out fear; because fear hath torment. He that feareth is not made perfect in love." 1 John 4:18. An intercessor must be totally and completely free of all fear. We must believe GOD is who He says He is and He can do what He says He can do. No if, ands, or buts about it. As an intercessor, we are called to battle on the front line at all times, and if the enemy even smells fear on us at any time, he will try and destroy us. The good news is, if we, as intercessors wear the correct garments and feed on the proper nourishment, we can rest assured that we will always be the victor. For it is written, "we are more than conquerors through Him who loved us." Romans 8:38.

The Bible requires all who belong to God to walk by faith and teaches us the definition of faith. The scripture reads, "Faith is the substance of things hoped for and the evidence of things not seen." Hebrews 11:1. If you claim to have the gift of faith, but you cannot stand in that faith, that faith is deficient. It will not and cannot produce for you. As is stated in the following two verses of scripture, "faith worketh by love, and without faith, we cannot even please God." Galatians 5:6 and Hebrews 11:6. Wow! What an awesome revelation that the body of Christ must grasp in order to even begin to develop a relationship with God. Without this revelation on faith, there can be no ministry, least of all the ministry of intercession. The Bible is very clear on the fact that without faith we cannot please God. The scripture reads, "But without faith it is impossible to please him; for he that cometh to

God must believe that he is, and that he is a rewarder of them that diligently seek him" Hebrews 11:6. The Word goes on to tell us that "whatsoever is not of faith is sin." Romans 14:23. So, we learn that since faith worketh by love, and when we do not walk in love, then we are not pleasing God no matter what else we may be doing for the kingdom of God. So, again, we see an example of how one garment cannot survive without the other. In other words, one without the other results in the intercessor being partially dressed. God has given each one of us a measure of faith. It is up to us to let God develop and grow that faith in us. We are constantly being brought into situations where we can choose to believe GOD and stand in faith or we can choose to murmur and complain and doubt God. If we choose to stand in faith, believing, each time we are faced with a test or trial, our faith will develop and grow stronger over time. Consequently, if we make the choice to doubt and complain, our faith will begin to wither and return back to where it started or the evil spirit of fear will replace it.

Fear in any form is an attack of the enemy. The Bible tells us that God has not given us the spirit of fear but of power, and of love, and of a sound mind. This is telling us that if we are operating out of fear instead of faith, we are not operating with the mind of Christ as the scripture commands us to do. So if we are not operating with the mind of Christ then we are leaning to our own understanding and is in complete disobedience to the Word and the will of Almighty God. If we're in disobedience, then we cannot get our prayers answered; hence, the ministry of intercession is of no effect. As a result, the intercessor is missing a very important garment from the required garments of an effective intercessor.

When God commands us to walk by faith and not by sight, He is well aware of how tremendously difficult that can be for us when everything around us is screaming at us to believe what we see with our natural eyes. 2 Corinthians 9:7 He is also aware that we cannot keep this commandment without Him. This is precisely the reason He commands us in the Book of John to be in Him and He in us. The scripture reads,

"Abide in me, and I in you. As the branch cannot bear fruit of itself, except it abide in the vine no more can ye, except ye abide in love. I am the vine, ye are the branches He that abideth in me, and I in him the same bringeth forth much fruit: for without me ye can do nothing." John 15:4–5.

With this said, it behooves us to take heed and totally yield to the leading of the Holy Spirit in every area of our lives. Of course, being human, we could be tricked into falling for the lie of the enemy concerning not having to ask God with certain decisions. He is very astute at trying to get to believe that we know what to do on our own in various situations that will present themselves from time to time. He would like for us to think that if we did it a certain way before, we can do it that same way again. Big, big lie. If we can remember to always check with the Lord, it would save us a lot of time and a lot of heartache. Since most people are the same, we all get duped more times than not. It seems to take us quite a few times to train ourselves to just yield, submit, and inquire of God with not just occasional decisions but with every decision. Once we get this and begin to walk in trust, and walk in faith, we soon learn just how pleasing it is to Him.

We must accept the fact that there will never ever come a time when we can assess a situation and/or can discern a situation on our own. Only God knows everything there is to know for the present or future. Only God has the capability of being able to know the ending from the beginning. The scripture reads, "Declaring the end from the beginning, and from ancient times the things that are not yet done saying, My counsel shall stand, and I will do all my pleasure". Isaiah 46:10. There will still be times even after we've taken the time to pray and inquire of God that everything will not necessarily immediately look as if it agrees with the Word from God; hence, we will have to walk it out by faith. If He says no, then it is no, but if He says yes, then it is yes no matter what it looks like. This is the kind of faith that caused Abel, Enoch, Noah, and Abraham, just to mention a few of the Old Testament saints to be singled out by God Himself to be considered faithful. They are called by name in the Bible and were declared to have obtained a good report from the Lord because of their faith. The scripture reads,

> "By faith Abel offered unto God a more excellent sacrifice than Cain, by which he obtained witness that he was righteous, God testifying of his gifts: and by it he being dead yet speaketh. By faith Enoch was translated that he should not see death, and was not found, because God had translated him for before his translation he had this testimony, that he pleased God. ... By faith Noah, being warned of God of things not seen as yet, moved with fear, prepared an ark to the saving of his house, by the which he condemned the world, and became heir of the righteousness which is by faith. By faith Abraham, when he was called to go out into a place which he should after receive for an inheritance, obeyed, and he went out not knowing whither he went." Hebrews 11:4–8.

This shows us how so very important and pleasing it is to God to walk in faith. The scripture declares to us that these saints died in faith, not having received the promises, but having seen then afar off. Hebrews 11:13

We have come into a time in the earth where the enemy is taking over to the point of commandeering people's minds and bombarding them with evil thoughts and causing them to perform evil acts. In order to combat the enemy, we have to first come to the realization that it is the enemy that is perpetrating the evil. Next, we have to prepare ourselves for battle by learning about our weapon which is the Word of God. Once we know what the weapon is, we then begin training ourselves on the correct way to utilize it. Finally, we get ourselves to the point of using our weapon on a daily by reading and speaking the Word of God over every situation. Moreover, we must remember that this weapon will only work if we believe it. Therefore, we must walk by faith. In addition to faith, this weapon will not work properly without love. For faith worketh by love.

The garment of integrity is a quality or qualities that are exhibited in the day to day life situations of people when they think no one is watching. "Who shall ascend into the hill of the Lord? Or who shall stand in His holy place? He that hath clean hands, and pure heart; who hath not lifted up his soul unto vanity, nor sworn deceitfully." Psalms 24:5–6. I know we all believe that we are the poster child for integrity, but how do we manifest that integrity. Can we be trusted to display it on our jobs? Are we really giving our best and working as unto the Lord when our boss is not around? Can we be trusted when we're alone at home? You know, what about those unspoken thoughts of our hearts? These are the things that God sees. What will you change if you realize others are watching you? Can anyone of us immediately answer with a resounding Nothing? If a man is not trusted with that which belongs to another, how can he be trusted with his own. The scripture reads, "If therefore ye have not been faithful in the unrighteous mammon, who will commit to your trust the true riches? And if ye have not been faithful in that which is another man's, who shall give you that which is your own?" Luke 16:11–12.

The reason the Lord called David a man after His own heart

is because of David's heart of integrity. When you study David's life in the Bible, you come to realize that David is a man who was loyal, who could be trusted in his decisions, and a man of mercy. For example, David refused to kill the man that hunted him to kill him for many years. He had several opportunities to kill King Saul, but refused to dishonor God and kill the one that was put in place by God. He would rather be pleasing to God. On another occasion, David proved his integrity when he remembered his covenant with Jonathan, the son of the man that was trying to kill him. After, he became king, he brought Jonathan's only living child and his family into the palace and made sure that he not only lived in the palace, but also ate at the kings table for every meal. 2 Samuel 9:7.

Further evidence of integrity is reflected when, we, the saints of God, are being careful what we allow ourselves to meditate on. This includes what we watch, what we listen to, and what we talk about. When we allow ungodly, worldly things to occupy our thoughts, we become hardened and callous to the things of God. The Anointing on a person is beautiful because people see Jesus and Jesus is Beautiful which is one of His attributes. In order for the people of God, the church, to be a part of what God is doing in the earth with the end time revival that is taking place right now, we have to go to another level, a higher level in God in the Spirit. People are not going to stay in our churches if we are not moving with the Holy Spirit–the Holy Ghost. There are people currently sitting in the pews that are already at a high level in God, and they are not going to stay in places where the intercessors and the Pastors are not growing–going higher. To know God and to love God with all our hearts, with all of our minds, and with all of our souls is always a necessity whatever our calling, but especially for the calling of intercessor. To know that God is who He says that He is and to know that He will do what He said He would do is the foundation of an intercessor. To know that He is perfect, that His Word is true, and that He cannot fail, and that He is the greatest of all is the lifeline of an intercessor. To reiterate, an intercessor must be totally and completely free of all fear. As intercessors, we must walk in this kind of unwavering belief and intimate knowledge that whatever God says is so. No if, ands, or buts about it. As intercessors, we are always out in front forging a path in the spirit, and if the enemy even smells fear on us at any time, he will try and destroy us immediately. The good news is, if we as intercessors wear the correct garments and feed on the proper nourishment, we can rest assured that we will always be the victor. For it is written, we are more than conquerors through Him who loved us. So, let's get dressed and go to battle!

Chapter Sixteen

REVERENTIAL FEAR

"And fear not them which kill the body, but are not able to kill the soul: but rather fear Him which is able to destroy both soul and body in hell." Matthew 10:28. KJV. "Be not afraid of them that kill the body, and after that have no more that they can do. But I will forewarn you whom ye shall fear. Fear Him, which after He hath killed hath power to cast into hell, yea, I say unto you, Fear Him." Luke 12:4–5.

J T IS INCREASINGLY evident that more and more people do not possess the reverential fear of God as the Bible teaches. An audacious lack of reverence is being manifested both inside and outside of the church. Shockingly, there are a large majority of us who are professing to be born again Christians living in situations that are clearly forbidden in the Word of God. We are making up our own rules as we go, and are citing the world's views as our guide. This pervasive lack of reverential fear for the Lord is putting a very large number of the church and the world in very precarious positions. For God will not be mocked and whatever seeds we sow with our beliefs and lifestyles will come back upon us as the scripture declares. The scripture reads, "Be not deceived; God is not mocked: for whatsoever a man soweth, that shall he also reap." Galatians 6:7. As scripture has taught us from Genesis to Revelation, through which God, Himself, has made abundantly clear, He will not share His glory with anyone at any time. The scripture goes on to teach that whoever is a friend of the world is an enemy to God. Thereby, it behooves us all to be very mindful of our approach to God and to His commandments. The scripture reads, "It is a fearful thing to fall into the hands of the living God". Hebrews 10:31. Whether we like it or not or even understand it or not, God has put into writing His commandments that must be kept by all generations. We hear people from time to time try and convince us that the Old Testament scripture does not apply to us today in order to excuse certain sins. There are even some that will try and convince the body of Christ that there is particular scripture in the Word of God that is not true. It's impossible to believe some of the Bible if not all. It is also impossible to have the New Testament without the Old Testament. All real Bible readers/students know that it is impossible for someone to have one without the other, and they know that such a premise is total fabrication. All who makes such false declarations are revealing that they have not and do not read or study the Bible for themselves. Jesus clearly teaches that not one Word of the scripture shall go unfulfilled. And we learn while studying the scripture that people have been trying to do things their own way from the beginning of time with disastrous results.

Let's begin by taking a look at the children of Israel as Moses was attempting to lead them out of Egypt into the promised land. The children of Israel, after ten different instances of disobedience and unbelief, failed to reach the Promise Land that God had prepared for them. The scripture reads,

"Because all those men which have seen my
glory, and my miracles, which I did in Egypt

99

and in the wilderness, and have tempted me now these ten times, and have not hearkened to my voice, Surely, they shall not see the land which I swear unto their fathers, neither shall any of them that provoked me see it. But my servant Caleb, because he had another spirit with him, and hath followed me fully, him will I bring into the land whereunto he went, and his seed shall possess it." Numbers 14:22–24.

Because they refused to adhere to God's commandments, they turned an eleven-day journey into a forty-year disastrous trek through the wilderness without ever seeing or claiming what belonged to them as God had promised their forefathers before them. We read the account of this unfinished journey and think to ourselves that this would not have ever happened to us. We also tell ourselves that we would have been obedient and believed God. I hate to be the bearer of bad news, but we would not have behaved any differently than the Hebrew children. The reason that I know this to be so is because we are doing the exact same thing today. We are adding extra time onto our individual journeys and are going around in circles in one or more areas of disobedience. It could be pride, lack of forgiveness, offense, anger, etc. We know exactly what it is and so does God. We are wondering what is taking God so long to answer our prayers. Guess what, God is waiting on us to get our acts together. He's waiting for us to obey and get that thing right that He spoke to us about twenty years ago. Surprise, God wins! We cannot out wait Him!

Amazingly, we spend so much time rationalizing our disobedience instead of yielding, submitting, and repenting. Our flesh convinces us that if we just throw ourselves into some other work for God, He will somehow forget what He has commanded us to get straightened out. Sorry, been there! Tried that! Take my word for it, it doesn't work! Waste of time! Again, I reiterate, He wins! As scripture shows us, the Hebrew children not only wasted forty years, but they did not make it out alive. The scripture reads, "For the Lord had said of them, They shall surely die in the wilderness. And there was not left a man of them, save Caleb the son of Jephunneh, and Joshua the son of Nun." Numbers 26:65. So, please, fear God and obey Him so we can get on with taking our rightful place in the kingdom. So we can take that place of authority and command the demonic forces as we were created to do. We were left in charge!

Just in case you're not convinced that God means business, let's take a look at the story of Ananias and Sapphira in the Book of Acts. This couple decided to choose to test God instead of walking in the fear and reverence of God. They conspired to lie to the apostles concerning money for the price of some land that was sold. They wanted to appear to be more generous than they actually were and lied concerning the total amount of the sale. They both were instantly killed when confronted by the apostles. They paid a very, very high price. Peter told them both prior to their deaths that they lied to the Holy Spirit. The scripture reads, "But Peter said, Ananias why hath Satan filled thine heart to lie to the Holy Ghost, and to keep back part of the price of the land? Acts 5:3. We learned from that tragic story that God knows all and sees all. I believe this story also exposed the true motivation for Ananias and Sapphira's giving. They were more interested in impressing the apostles and the people than they were concerning the giving to further the kingdom of God. Just as Ananias and his wife's true intents were clearly known by God, so are the motivations and intents of our hearts lay bare before the Lord. Again, don't waste your precious time! He already knows. So in reverential fear, let's intentionally yield and submit. Let's intentionally obey. Let's say, yes Lord, here am I, send me. The above illustrations of willful disobedience and testing of God are just two of the instances from the Bible where that kind of behavior ended with disastrous results. There are many more stories that can and will further illustrate that it is a very dangerous stance to take the mercy and grace of God for granted. Please do not take the grace of God for granted!

The more people are influenced by worldly views, the more the church is being lured into believing that a casual, disobedient approach to the things of God are okay with God. I mean this both figuratively and literally. The saints of God are not honoring God and showing Him the reverential fear that He's commanded. First of all, a large number of people are treating God as if He's some big ATM in the sky. They only call on Him to fulfill some physical or financial need from time to time. When they get their prayers answered, they push Him to the back of their lives until the next crisis arise. Until a need arises, they appear to be very comfortable living in what the Bible calls sin. This casual attitude is also being reflected in our giving, our prayer time, and in the way we present ourselves to God. Next, I want to focus on a pet peeve of mine, which is how we seem to get more and more casual in our dress when we go to the house of God. I've observed that a lot of saints come into the house of God without putting very much thought into who they are coming to worship. They do not even give God the same consideration as they do their jobs. But, they are very cognizant to adhere to the dress code that their respective jobs dictate. There is scripture that clearly shows God requirements for His priest to dress before coming before Him. The scripture reads, "And the cloths of service, and the holy garments for Aaron the priest, and the garments of his sons, to minister in the priest's office." Exodus 31:10. Are we not called the redeemed kings and priests unto our God by the shed blood of our Lord and Savior Jesus Christ. The scripture reads,

"For thou wast slain, and hast redeemed us to God by thy blood out of every kindred, and tongue, and people, and nation; And hast made us unto our God kings and priests, and we shall reign on the earth." Revelation 5:9–10. I personally believe that how you prepare yourself for presentation before someone is reflective of how you really feel about that person. Personally, I want the world and whomever else that's watching to see, for me, there is no greater one to go before or no greater place to go to be in the presence of this person, almighty God. The average person in this nation if had the opportunity to visit the White House and meet the President, would put on their personal best. In case we don't realize it, when going to the house of God, we're going to a house that is far greater than the White House, and we're going to meet someone who's far greater than the President. Yes, when we visit the White House, we will leave with a good temporary memory that will only last for this earthly life span, but when we visit the church house, we leave with a forever memory that will last for an eternity, spanning this earthly life time into the next life. I'm well aware that a lot of people don't have access to nice clothing, and they have to wear what they currently possess. I do understand that fact, and I know God understands as well. So, no, I'm not advocating for everyone to be dressed up in the church, but I am advocating for everyone to be their best and to bring their best when presenting themselves before the best.

Chapter Seventeen

PERSEVERANCE

"And let us not be weary in well doing: for in due season we shall reap, if we faint not." Galatians 6:9

JESUS SAID, "No man, having put his hand to the plough, and looking back, is fit for the kingdom of God." Luke 9:62. Most of us saints, if asked, would be quick to assure others that we would stay the course in our walk with the Lord no matter the circumstance. And we would be sincere in our declaration of loyalty until we hit that hard patch in our walk that doesn't align itself with how we thought our walk should be. Yes, it is very understandable to have a desire to pull back when things seem to go awry, but we must not give in to that desire and stay the course until the job is completed. Consequently, this is an opportunity to reach deep down inside and hold steadfast to what we believe. This is the time to exercise perseverance the most in the body of Christ. For the saints of God who refuses to give up or give in, there can only be victory no matter the origin or caliber of the attacks of the enemy. Every promise that our God has made shall come to pass regardless of what else has happened along the way.

Often times, we're really running into the roadblocks because

God is getting ready to do something awesome in our lives. The turbulence we're experiencing is because the enemy is trying to sabotage God's plans. The enemy relishes every opportunity to try and cause us to abort our blessings. The scripture teaches us that it is always the darkest before the dawn. Every serious walk with the Lord will go through a battery of tests. The Word on the inside of us will be severely tested as well as our faith in God. This is when we hold on for dear life. I cannot say enough about perseverance. It is one of the most important garments that an intercessor can wear. It is so necessary in receiving anything from God, in overcoming the enemy, and in walking in victory in every area. Without the garment of perseverance, all the other garments will be deficient. You see, the enemy's strategy is designed to wear the saint of God down, to make us give up and give in. He tries to so bombard us to the point of exhaustion. His desired goal is for us to just throw in the towel. This is especially true in the prayer life of the intercessor when the more we pray, the worse things seem to become. The enemy's ultimate plan is for us to lose all hope and cease to pray. We must never stop praying, especially, when we can't see anything or it looks as if nothing at all is happening. This is the time to for us to pray the Word of God while simultaneously speaking what we want to come to pass and keep speaking it for as long as it takes for it to manifest. We must keep this up until we receive our petition even if it takes weeks, months, or even years. This is also the time to, maybe, add fasting to our prayers. The scripture teaches us as follows, "And when he was come into the house, his disciples asked him privately, Why could not we cast him out? And he said unto them, This kind can come forth by nothing, but by prayer and fasting." Mark 9:28–29. The gift of the spirit of perseverance is one of the reasons the enemy hate intercessors. This same analogy applies to each and every required garment of the intercessor. In actuality, no one garment can survive or produce without the other.

If you are called to intercede then you've already or rather always have encountered the unusual attacks from the enemy because praying for the kingdom and saints of God is the very last thing the enemy wants us to do. In all of scripture, one of the requirements for all saints from the Old and New Testament have been and still is to endure various situations, circumstances, trials, and tribulations. Children of God, especially intercessors are asked to endure on a long-term basis through life situations that can appear unsurmountable and impossible. Situations that require perseverance in order to make it from day to day. Because we live in a fallen world, Christians do not get a free pass and have to endure various life situations just as does the world. In other words, being a Christian does not exempt us from experiencing, at some point in time, stressful and sometimes devastating life situations. The thing that distinguishes the Christian from the world is in how we go through the various life situations that will eventually affect all in some way, either directly or indirectly.

Perseverance and endurance is especially needed in the ministry of intercession due to the very nature of the ministry. Sometimes, an intercessor is required to persist in prayer until there is a sign or word from God to discontinue praying. We must keep going until the job is done whether one hour, one day, one week, or even one year. As we can see, an intercessor must not be easily distracted. We must be thoroughly focused and persistent individuals who take the assignment to pray for someone very, very seriously. You see, the prayers of an intercessor could be for a city, an individual, or for a particular situation that is life threatening as is referenced in the book of Ezekiel when God looked for a man/woman to stand in the gap for an entire city so that He would not have to destroy it. In other words, persistence and endurance in prayer is of the utmost importance.

In a world that is anti-God and anti-Christian, we, the body of Christ and especially the intercessor will have to muster every ounce of perseverance we possibly can in order to successfully combat the evil spirits that are being unleashed against the Body in this hour. We have to be especially careful to remember that we wrestle not against flesh and blood, but against principalities, against powers, against the rulers of the darkness of this world, against spiritual wickedness in high places. Ephesians 6:12 We have to also remember to stay connected to the vine—the Lord Jesus Christ—because the enemy's intention is to steal, kill, and destroy. John 10:10 Those that endure to the end shall be saved. Matthew 24:13. We are asked to persevere and endure because the attacks of the enemy can become overwhelming in the natural if we forget that we are in Christ Jesus and He is in us. John 15:4 You see, we still have a significant role to play in the upkeep of our relationship with God after we accept Christ and is saved and filled with the Holy Spirit. In addition, we have to keep in mind who we are and whose we are at all times. We have to daily walk in this knowledge as well because faith without works is dead. James 2:28

Jesus persevered to make it to the cross. He rejoiced the night of His betrayal at the prospect of sharing the Passover with the disciples earlier in the evening because He knew that He had persevered and endured and completed His assignment in the earth. He endured and made it to the destination without sin so that we could be saved and become sons of God. He came, lived, and died without sin or compromise which gave Him the victory over the grave. The Bible teaches us that Jesus was tempted in all points without sin. The scripture reads, "For we have not an high priest which cannot be touched with the feeling of our infirmities;

but was in all points tempted like as we are, yet without sin." Hebrews 4:15. He also conquered death and the grave. He proved His victory by doing what He said by coming out of the grave after three days and three nights with all power and all authority over all the power of the enemy. He, in turn, commissioned us and have given us all power over all power of the enemy in His name (in the name of Jesus).

In order for the people of God, the church, to be a part of what God is doing in the earth through the various ministries, we must to persevere to go to that higher level in God that is attained by and through the Spirit of God. People are very hungry for the supernatural and are looking in places that are not moving with the Holy Spirit. There cannot be people sitting in the pews that are already at a higher level in God than the leadership. This is one of the major reasons that people are not staying in churches where the intercessors and the pastors are not growing and going higher in God. We must be practice what we preach because there is a hungry world out there that is searching for God even if they don't realize it just yet.

As intercessors, we must persevere in prayer, believing, that our prayers are going to be answered, if for no other reason, just because we're praying according to God's Word and in faith. It's time out for saints spending hours and hours praying wondering if God is going to answer. We have to step it up because the enemy is certainly upping his game. We must always pray with confidence that every prayer is heard and every prayer is answered. It is a waste of our time if we are praying without faith and participating in a guessing game as to whether God will answer our prayers. We're wasting our time and the time of the people that we're supposedly praying for. Our prayers must be established on some foundational things such as: God cannot lie, God's Word will not return unto Him void, God is a rewarder of them that diligently seeks Him. A person that is without the Lord Jesus Christ and the Holy Spirit is much worse than a person that is going to court without a witness and without a lawyer—defenseless. But with Jesus Christ and the Holy Spirit, we cannot lose because we have an irrefutable witness. We have a lawyer that cannot lose a case, a witness that cannot lie, and as a bonus, we have an advocate that is willing to and have already gone before us—even in our places so we don't ever have to go.

A lot of intercessors or saints of God spend a great deal of or the bulk of their Christian life waiting for things to get or be just right before stepping out and doing the will of God and to bring souls into the kingdom, etc. When difficult situations arise in our lives, we spend a whole lot of time crying out to God for help and running from the fight instead of running to the fight or battle as victors are supposed to do. We should know our God as David did and know that He will never leave nor forsake us no matter what it looks like or no matter what the lying enemy says. We should realize that running to the battle or fight is the only way that our God can show Himself strong on our behalf. We must also realize that as long as we are on this earth, there will always be good and not so good occurring, simultaneously, in our lives. It is up to us whose report we will believe. Will we run from the giants or to the giants? Will we persevere and possess the land or will we tremble in fear and call ourselves grasshoppers—the name the enemy wants us to receive? It's up to us to make the choice! God is waiting!

Chapter Eighteen

OBEDIENCE

Though He were a Son yet learned He obedience by the things which He suffered; Hebrews 5:8

SADLY, TODAY, WE are witnessing an unprecedented onslaught of willful disobedience to the Word of God. Purposeful and willful disobedience is being perpetuated at a pace that cannot be compared to anything that we have witnessed in our lifetime. As a result, the condition of the earth can only be compared to what we have read about in the Bible before the birth of Jesus. With our own eyes, we're watching sin and evil wreak carnage on the world at breakneck speed. Consequently, we, the body of Christ are at a loss for what to do when we, supposedly, have so many intercessors already praying. We are wondering, how could this be happening on our watches? We are wondering, how could so many people be so deceived in the earth today? Unfortunately, the answer is because the church has failed in its assignment. The church has grown very weak due to being lured off course, especially, in the last twenty years. The enemy cleverly instigated the church to begin focusing on the number of people in attendance instead of the number of souls being brought into the kingdom of God. As a result of getting into an unspoken competition with other churches with church growth, we have softened our message in order to try and prevent people from leaving. Consequently, people are being lulled to sleep by the enemy due to a lack of the Word. In return, we are reaping a mass disobedience to the Word of God in the church as it is in the world. How can we as the church provide a godly example to the world when we are in the same predicament or worse? We can pray around the clock, twenty-four hours a day to no avail, if we are in disobedience to the Word ourselves. Our prayers will not be answered. We cannot live in disobedience and expect to receive anything from God.

The Lord Jesus, before going to be with the Father, promised us that He would pray the Father to send us a helper—the Holy Spirit. We need the Holy Spirit in order to fulfill our purpose in this earth. The scripture teaches us that God has given the gift of the Holy Spirit to those that obey Him. Obedience is of the utmost importance to God. When we are commanded to walk in obedience to God, this includes those times when things that we are told to do does not make any sense, whatsoever, to our natural minds. When the things that we are commanded to do seem to be totally unrelated to the situation at hand. This also includes those times when we have experienced a devastating loss of some kind, and we're trying to hold on for dear life. There is no excuse for disobedience, ever, whatever the circumstance. When things are crazy, it serves to let us know of a surety whether or not we trust in God as we have been professing. It's very easy to declare our faith and undying love for the Lord when things are going along fine or when we're on our proverbial mountain tops. Complete unreserved obedience to God is an absolute must for an intercessor at all times and in all circumstances. Obedience to God is a direct connection to our faith in God. Obedience is also an indication of how much of our flesh is still alive or how much has been brought down. Obedience to the commandments of God is the way we prove our love for Him. The scripture reads,

"He that hath my commandments, and keepeth them, he it is that loveth me, and he that loveth me shall be loved of my Father, and I will love him, and will manifest myself to him. John 14:21. "JESUS answered and said unto him, if a man love me, he will keep my words and my Father will love him, and we will come unto him and make our abode with him. He that loveth me not keepth not my sayings and the word which ye hear is not mine but the Father's which sent me." John 14:23-24 The scripture goes on to tell us that we can have the confidence that God will hear and answer our prayers if we are in obedience to Him. "And whatsoever we ask, we receive of Him, because we keep His commandments, and do those things that are pleasing in His sight." 1 John 3:22.

As the Bible teaches us from Genesis to Revelation, walking in complete obedience to God is not an easy walk. In fact, it can be very difficult as Abraham can attest when he was asked by God to sacrifice his long awaited, miracle son on the altar. It can also be a very lonely walk as is shown with the life of Noah. He was asked to build an ark that took many years to complete. As a result of his obedience, he had to suffer great ridicule and persecution. Moses is another example of someone obeying God in the midst of great resistance from both the Egyptians as well as the people that he was called to lead into the promised land. When you are determined to follow God with your whole heart, there will not be many people that will understand you even in your own household. Moses experienced this with both his sister Miriam and his brother Aaron to the point that God, Himself, had to intervene on Moses' behalf.

Our decision whether to be obedient or disobedient will define the direction and course of our lives and the lives of our families, forever. For instance, King Saul chose to disobey God and reaped the rewards of disobedience in his life and in the lives of his children forever. The scripture reads,

> "And Samuel said to Saul, Thou hast done foolishly: thou hast not kept the commandment of the LORD thy God, which He commanded thee: for now would the LORD have established thy kingdom upon Israel forever. But now thy kingdom shall not continue: the LORD hath sought him a man after his own heart and the LORD hath commanded him to be captain over His people, because thou hast not kept that which the LORD commanded thee." 1 Samuel 13:13–14.

Although all the promises of God are ours, we still have to do battle with the enemy to claim them and to walk in and to live in them. This is what God showed us with the Israelites. They were promised the land flowing with milk and honey, but they could not seem to overcome their willful disobedience to the commands of God. They delayed their journey through the wilderness because of stubbornness and disobedience. In fact, their willful refusal to follow God's commands caused all of them over the age of twenty to die in the wilderness before reaching the promised land. Even Moses was kept back because of disobedience. The importance of being obedient is of the utmost importance.

Even though we have the ability to defeat the plans of the enemy in the name of Jesus and receive and enjoy the promises of God, we have to first defeat and bring under subjection our own flesh and stubbornness. Although, the children of Israel's "*ites*" or obstacles to their pathway to receiving God's promises were currently occupying the land that was promised to them through Abraham, their biggest obstacle to overcome was their own disobedience and willful stubbornness. Although the current occupants were occupying land that did not belong to them in the natural, they were not going to vacate the land until they were forcibly removed by the children of Israel. God commissioned Moses and the children of Israel to go in and claim their land. In order to claim their God-given land, they had to engage in battle to it. The land was being occupied by the Canaanites, Hittites Amorites, Hivites, and Jebusites, and they had to be removed. The scripture reads,

> "And it shall be when the LORD shall bring thee into the land of the Canaanites, and the Hittites, and the Amorites, and the Hivites, and the Jebusites, which He sware unto thy fathers to give thee, a land flowing with milk and honey, that thou shalt keep this service in this month." Exodus 13:5.

This is the very same way it is with our promises from God, whether it's our healing, our finances, or our family's salvation. We have to fight and defeat the enemy beginning with our own hearts and minds and will. No, we do not fight in the natural nor do we fight alone, but we fight in the name of Jesus and with the power of the Holy Spirit. Sometimes, even in our obedience to the Lord, we need to cry out to God for help.

What we have to remember, here, is that our weapons are not carnal but mighty through God and since our battles are not with flesh and blood but is against principalities and powers and rulers of darkness of this world, against spiritual wickedness in high places, we must put on the whole armor of God: truth, righteousness, gospel of peace, faith, helmet of salvation and the sword of the Spirit which is the word of God. But none of this armor will work if we are walking in disobedience to God. In order to be victorious and pleasing to God, which will enable us to defeat our enemies within and without, we must be in total obedience to God, not just some of the time, but all of the time and in all the areas of our lives.

Chapter Nineteen

ANSWERED PRAYER

*"I exhort therefore, that, first of all, supplications, prayers,
intercessions, and giving of thanks, be made for all men;"*
1 Timothy 2:1

*"And this is the confidence that we have in him, that,
if we ask any thing according to his will, he heareth us:
And if we know that he hear us, whatsoever we ask, we
know that we have the petitions that we desired of him."*
1 John 5:14–15

OW TO SUCCEED in getting prayers answered in the body
of Christ and the ministry of intercession? Sadly, this is
a question that is being asked in the body of Christ now
more than at any other time in recent memory. Fortunately, there
is an answer, and it's a multifaceted answer that is applicable to
every saint whether or not he or she is called to the ministry of
intercession. There are several factors that have been touched
upon in *Commanding the Forces* that warrants a revisit in order to
adequately answer the aforementioned question. The answer is
predominantly centered around and involve the personal aspects
of our ministries.

We must begin by emphasizing that an intercessor must be aware of the tactics of the enemy by staying in tune to the Holy Spirit. In order to be able to adequately recognize the tactics of the enemy, we must have an intimate knowledge of the Word of God. We must be versed in the Word to the point of not needing to track down our Bibles every time we're battling the enemy. By daily studying the Word of God, we will be able to hear and, readily, recognize the voice of God with more accuracy. Because we will be able to readily recognize the voice of God, we immediately know when something comes to us that is contrary to the Word of God. Knowing the Word of God will also guarantee that we will pray the will of God accurately. When we pray the will of God in faith, our prayers will always be answered. In addition, there will be times when we are being prayed for or is praying for someone when we will encounter turbulence in our lives and situations and in the lives of the ones we're praying for. This is due to a push back and resistance from the enemy. This is where the intercessor should double down and press through. Unfortunately, this is the point more than any other that causes a large majority of intercessors to back off and begin to doubt and question both God and their callings. This is not the time to lose faith, but it is the time to walk by faith and not by sight. This is the time to be steadfast and become even more tenacious in our praying. When turbulence comes as a result of prayer, it is a sure indication that God is at work in our lives and in our situations. We have to continue to give God all the praise, the glory and the honor. Amen! Although an intercessor is a fighter—created that way by God—we must have the wisdom and discernment to pick our fights. This is so important. In other words, there are some things that will come against us that we should not even waste the time or the energy on because it is sent from the enemy as a distraction from the real fight.

Sometimes when we begin to pray, we will be bombarded with a lot of non-essential, worldly, and carnal thoughts. First of all, we have to realize that we are under attack from the enemy to try and waste our time and to distract us from the task at hand which is prayer. At these times when we become cognizant of the enemy's tactics, we must take authority over our thoughts by praying in tongues and quoting the scripture that deals directly with our circumstances. I realize at times we are convinced that our particular situations are not covered in the Bible. I can assure you, it is covered in the Word of God, just keep reading. As we know, the Bible teaches us there is nothing too hard for God. Consequently, we must constantly practice the Word, and we must accurately discern the Word of God as we continue to grow as a result of our study and research. In getting our prayers answered, we have to always, always walk in total obedience to God to the best of our ability. As we already know, we are to never, ever think we know what to do without going to God and asking for direction. We are to never take for granted that we understand what to do on our own. We must let the Holy Spirit lead us at all times.

As an intercessor and a child of God, we can learn a lesson from two characters that are depicted in the Bible—David in the book of 2 Samuel and the ant from the book of Proverbs on how to approach their life situation, overcome any obstacle, and reign victorious. When we study about these characters that are of different species and have different overall goals, we still become aware that they have something in common. I believe we will see some important characteristics that was common in each and was instrumental in them accomplishing their goals. When we take a deeper look, we realize that, amazingly, neither of the characters feared the size of their enemies or prey. They both approached each situation knowing who they were, and each knew what they were equipped with, and each of them knew how to use what they had with strategy and wisdom. Very, very important assets. The similarities of these two distinct species as depicted in the Bible is amazing. It teaches us that if God be for us, we can do anything if we stay in faith, know who we are in God, and ask God for wisdom. There is nothing impossible with God. When going through a trial or time of testing, we must strive with all of our hearts and might to stay close to or come even closer to God than ever before. We must do this—this is so important! In fact, this is of the utmost importance in getting our petitions met! We must keep a constant check on our heart conditions, our motivations, our intentions at all times and especially during the times of testing and trial. We must always stay in a repentant mode. This entails always being ready and willing to repent of any sin and immediately ask GOD to remove all unforgiveness, offense, and disobedience from our hearts and life. We must walk in perfect love. We must strive for it with every fiber of our being and obey GOD explicitly and expediently! An intercessor, as a child of God, is told to put on the whole armor of God because our war is to be fought in the spiritual realm. An intercessor is likened, in the natural, unto the CIA, Marines, or some specially trained fighting force that is sent in to do a job that no one else can get accomplished. We are the ones that has direct communication with the top—the one in control. Sometimes our greatest conversations with God is when we don't open our mouths, but just listen; when we are communing spirit to Spirit; when our hearts are wide open and transparent before God. An intercessor must take heart and not be easily offended because the greatest spiritual battles that we will encounter will not come from the world, but from those who are supposed to be our allies a lot of the times. Don't be shaken, just remember what Jesus said, persecutions must come. An intercessor has authority in the spiritual realm in Jesus name. Ezekiel 22:30–31. The closer an intercessor gets to God or rather the more an intercessor matures in the things of God, i.e., walking in love; walking in obedience; the more severe the attacks will be from the enemy. The good news is, the more mature the intercessor becomes, the more equipped he or she is to defeat the enemy in the name of Jesus.

As an intercessor, we have to be spiritually sharp, spiritually in tune, and spiritually aware of what's going on in the spiritual realm at all times. The only way to stay and/or be spiritually sharp and in tune spiritually is to stay in the presence of God. In order to stay in the presence of God, we must fast and pray continually. Some part of our day, every day, should be set aside and consecrated unto the Lord in order to be directed, strengthened, and assigned. This is our duty. Just as we would go and confer with our bosses on a secular job to get instructions, we must go to our ultimate boss every day to get instructions; otherwise, we will be leaning to our own understanding and flying by the seat of our pants—so to speak. This receipt of daily instructions includes reading the Word of God as well as just praying.

When we reach heaven, we are equipped to thwart the plan of the enemy to wreak havoc in our lives and the lives of others. As an intercessor, our words carry power, the very power of God. We have to be very careful of what comes out of our mouths. As intercessors, our words are very powerful weapons. We must be quick to repent if tricked by the enemy into saying something that we did not mean to say. When interceding, we must never be in a hurry because it takes time to get into the presence of God. As intercessors, we must protect the anointing and our minds (our thought lives) at all cost. We must be fighters and warriors. We must prefer others before ourselves. We cannot be people pleasers, but God pleasers only. An intercessor must be the one to initiate going without food for a time in order to hear clearly.

A routine practice of listening for and hearing the voice of God clearly in order to pray accurately has to be a goal that we go after with diligence and purpose daily. We must also show diligence in setting aside special prayer time as well as striving to stay in a prayer mode all day, every day. No, it's not easy, but the Word teaches us that we can do all things through Christ.

An intercessor cannot just be a person who is satisfied with just attending or having church only on Sundays and Wednesdays. We must have church every day—seven days a week. Since the average person cannot attend church seven days a week, then we must bring the church to us. This can be accomplished by watching Christian television, reading Christian books, watching Christian DVDs, listening to Christian CDs, Christian tapes, etc. And, of course, we must seek God as to what He is saying concerning reading and listening material outside of the Word of God. As intercessors, we have to constantly be aware of the things that will try and vie for our time with the Lord. An uncluttered mind and heart is a necessity whether interceding, speaking a word into or over someone, or taking authority over the enemy. Effective intercession is not just about taking authority in prayer by being loud and forceful, but it is more about whose prayers are getting heard and whose prayers are getting answered by God. Therefore, taking authority over our lifestyles which includes what's going on inside is just as important as what's going on outside. In order to ensure that the inside is in optimal condition for praying with authority, we must meet God's qualifications of purification, holiness, consecration, obedience, trustworthiness. There is a certain lifestyle, spiritual dress and purified sound that will penetrate the spiritual realm. An intercessor must learn persistence, perseverance, patience. We must walk by faith, trust, and confidence.

As an intercessor, we must always take the high road. We must never be a man pleaser and only strive to please God. We must never look to anyone else for approval but to God alone. This means as an intercessor, we might never get a thank you in the natural or we might never be known by man. We must determine in our minds, in our hearts, and in our spirits that we only want to please God. Thereby realizing that by pleasing God, we will most likely displease man. God's ways and thoughts are so much higher than ours, and He longs to answer all of our prayers, but He is a perfect God who is always a God of perfect order.

Chapter Twenty

WHAT'S IN YOUR MOUTH?

"Death and life are in the power of the tongue; and they that love it shall eat the fruit thereof."

IT IS VERY sobering to realize that we have the ability to either speak life or death over our own lives and the lives of our loved ones. We've become so accustomed to speaking whatever comes to mind so much so that it has become an intrinsic part of our nature. Subsequently, we experience a real culture shock when we're taught that we have to suddenly begin to be aware of every word we speak. As expected, this will require a very steep learning curve for a large majority of us in the body of Christ. We must begin to pay close attention to what we're saying because the Bible teaches that the power of death and life is in the tongue. We have to become responsible for what's going into our hearts and out of our mouths. And we have to begin speaking what God is speaking through His Word. Throughout the Bible, it has been taught to us as well as demonstrated for us the importance of what we allow to go into our hearts. It is very important because what goes into our hearts has a direct correlation to what comes out of our mouths. At this juncture in history and at a time like no other since the beginning of time, we, as born again Christians, must become more vigilant in our spiritual lives while being even more cognizant of our spiritual temperatures. In other words, we must know where we are in our walk with the Lord. We must know what we're setting into motion with the way we live our lives, and what we are creating with the words that are coming out of our mouths. In order to be aware of and stay abreast of our spiritual conditions, we must ask ourselves some very important questions such as, whose words are we speaking into the atmosphere? What kind of a future are we creating and putting into place with our mouths? What are we allowing into our hearts? What are we putting before our eyes? Who has been speaking into us? What have we been speaking over ourselves? Are we speaking life or death? The scripture reads, "Take heed therefore how ye hear: for whosoever hath, to him shall be given; and whosoever hath not, from him shall be taken even that which he seemeth to have." Luke 8:18. As we know, what comes out of us is what has been put into us either through own doing or through whomever we have allowed to speak into and over our lives. We cannot speak out life if we're only taking in death. Speaking life requires us to first be filled with life. Believe it or not, the answers to the, above, questions can be answered by, simply, looking around at our current situations and taking serious stock of our lives. Wherever we are and whatever path we're on right now is what we've spoken or meditated upon in our hearts in the past.

We, the body of Christ, have been given the ability and the authority to create the future that we desire for ourselves and our families. Of course, God is the final authority, but He has given us the authority to speak His Word in faith believing that whatsoever we say, it shall come to pass. The scripture reads,

> "For verily I say unto you, That whosoever shall
> say unto this mountain, Be thou removed, and be
> thou cast into the sea, and shall not doubt in his

heart, but shall believe that those things which he
saith shall come to pass, he shall have whatsoever
he saith." Mark11:23.

What we speak, believing, is what we will have. As the scripture
teaches, we are made in the image of God. The Bible also teaches
that we, as born again saints of God, would be able to do the same
works that Jesus did and even greater works. It also teaches us
that whatsoever we ask the Father in the name of Jesus it would
be given to us. We can only walk in the promises of God if we
truly believe the Word, and trust the Lord in all circumstances.
Since this requires us to be serious hearers and doers of the Word,
we are driven to get lost in our study of the word of God to the
point of being able to recite scripture from memory, daily. This
ability can only be acquired by a daily study (hearing, reading,
and praying) the Word of God. The more we study the Word,
the stronger we grow in faith; thereby, becoming more confident
in speaking the Word which enables us to take authority over the
enemy. This kind of confidence comes to fruition as we develop a
personal relationship with the Lord Jesus believing His promise
that He is the only way to the Father. We have to believe the Word
of God, totally. A personal relationship will enable us to go boldly
before the throne in the name of Jesus. When we have access to
the throne of God, we have access to all the power, the peace, the
joy, and the presence of God.

Even so, we must not be deceived into thinking we will never
experience opposition from the enemy just because we're obeying
the Word of God. At the onset, it is easy to begin speaking the
Word over our situations until that Word is tested. When the
persecution comes, we become distracted and begin speaking the
things that we don't want to come to pass and speaking things that
are contrary to the Word of God. This is exactly what the enemy
wants us to do. This is another one of those areas where the enemy

defeats us the most. As an intercessor, we should speak the word of God in every life situation and circumstance. This is so very important in the Christian walk because in the spoken Word is life. This is one of the most important and major aspects of the Christian walk that is being grossly neglected. In maintaining a successful spiritual walk with the Lord, we gather our strength, our wisdom, our favor, and our answers in prayer. Outside of this close relationship with the Lord, we will have just the opposite of what we desire. This is the main reason so many of us saints are perplexed as to why we are unable to move forward in our individual walks with the Lord, and are still as immature in the spirit as we were ten or fifteen years ago. The average one of us, Christians, will tell ourselves that we are doing everything the Word tells us to, such as living for the Lord, praying, paying tithes, and assembling ourselves together with other saints. Because we are doing what we believe is living right or as we've been taught is the Christian way, we are wondering what is going on with God. But, there are some basic things, we, as saints of God need to understand and set as our foundation. We need to know God's Word is true; God is who He says He is; He can do what He says He can do; God is not a man that He should lie; there is nothing too hard for God; and God is the greatest of all. The average one of us, saints, expect God to answer every prayer in the same way, at the same time every time. And, when God does not answer when and how we envisioned, we begin to doubt. When doubt and disbelief gets into the mix, it breeds fear. So instead of praying the Word of God, we begin to pray our thoughts or our doubts and even the enemy's lies. This is a sure fire way of not getting anything from God; thus, catapulting us into this vicious cycle of speaking doubt and questioning God. All of this is the direct result of fear because we have forgotten the negative words that we've just spoken over our particular situations. In other words, we're forgetting our mouths. As soon as we're inconvenienced or persecuted, we begin to speak without praying it through. We don't realize that any progress we might have made can either be solidified or totally wiped out by what comes out of our mouths concerning our situations. Especially in critical situations, we have to be very careful to try and remember to never speak from our minds but from our spirits only after hearing from God. Our minds will automatically defer to the natural realm instead of the supernatural realm. As born again Christians, deferring to the supernatural should be automatic. We have to get to the point where the supernatural realm is the natural place for us to retreat. Instead of complaining or murmuring, we are supposed to be calling into being what we desire. This has been promised to us as faith-filled, Word speaking saints of God. Promises for healing, financial blessings, family protection, deliverance are just a few of the many, many promises in the Word that belongs to the saints of God and can be realized by the very words we speak.

Commanding The Forces

"For though we walk in the flesh, we do not war after the flesh. (For the weapons of our warfare are not carnal, but mighty through God to the pulling down of strongholds;)

T HE SCRIPTURE READS, "For God so loved the world that He gave His only begotten Son, that whosoever believeth in Him should not perish, but have everlasting life." John 3:16. As a result, a free gift of salvation has been given to the world, but the world doesn't know anything about it. Even though it has been placed within their reach, they cannot access it because of the scales upon their eyes. No matter how long the earth will remain, there can never be anything done to exceed or replicate the most awesome and most wonderful feat ever accomplished in and for the world. We, the body of Christ, have been chosen to be made privy to this most amazing and most awesome thing, and we have also been given the privilege to go into all places to teach and spread this good news. We have also been given the responsibility to be a representative of our Lord and Savior Jesus Christ in every arena of our lives. We have been entrusted with something wonderful that can be life-altering for all who desire and receive it. Because of the love of God for us while we were yet sinners, He has done this great thing that can never be surpassed! All that call on the name of the Lord shall be saved, and as a result will be given the ability to know, see, and hear the living God. We, as born again Christians, have been given this privilege by way of the shed blood of His Only Begotten Son, the Lord Jesus Christ. As called ministers of intercession and called saints of God, we have been given a mandate to go and teach and share this with all nations, baptizing them in the name of the Father, the Son, and the Holy Ghost. We are commanded to preach this good news, this gospel to every creature. In the name of Jesus, the name that is above every name, we've been given the authority to do the same works as He did while in the earth. As a result, we have been given the authority to cast out demons, lay hands on the sick and they shall recover, and speak those things that be not as though they are. In other words, we, as born again Christians, have been put in charge in Jesus' name. We are to occupy in the earth until He comes again. We're the ones that have received the promise of the Holy Spirit from the Father to be witnesses of Jesus in the earth. In other words, we are in command! As intercessors, we have been endowed by the Almighty God to stand in the gap for and cover His people in prayer. We have been given the authority to call into being the Word of God. As saints of God, especially, those of us who are called to intercede, have been given the authority to stand in the gap for our families and others. Because the Lord Jesus prayed the Father to send the Holy Spirit, we have been given the power and authority to command the demonic forces in the name of Jesus just as Jesus did when in the earth. We can command the enemy to let God's people go and he has to obey. We can command God's people to be set free in the name of Jesus. In the name of Jesus, we have been endued with the same power and authority to heal people sick of various diseases. We have been given the same power and authority to cast down evil imaginations. In Jesus's name, we have been given the power to tread on serpents and scorpions. We have been given power over all the power of the enemy and nothing shall by any means hurt us. The spirits are subject unto us in the name of Jesus. In order for us to operate in this power that Jesus has given us, we must, first, love the Lord God with all of our hearts, and all of our souls, and with all of our strength, and with all of our minds, and love our neighbors as ourselves. By speaking the promises of God, we can claim our family members and others for the kingdom of God.

Why are we as the church allowing the world to set the bar and the standard for us? Surprisingly, the church and the body of Christ have been operating under an identity that has been given to us by the world. For some unknown reason, the world believes the saint of God should be this quiet, soft-spoken, fearful person who has no say in anything that goes on outside of the church building. This is a lie that has been fabricated by the enemy as he actively promotes his own evil agenda in the world. As the Bible tells us, we do not fight with flesh and blood people that we can see with our natural eyes, but we do fight against the spiritual forces behind the scenes that is influencing the people. The scripture reads, "For we wrestle not against flesh and blood, but against principalities against powers, against the rulers of the darkness of this world against spiritual wickedness in high places." Ephesians 6:12. In order to have a successful outcome in any battle (whether in the natural/physical or spiritual) we must use the correct weapons, weapons that have been tested. In the Bible, the story of David and Goliath references where the king tried to convince David to wear his armor to fight Goliath, but David refused because he had not tested the armor. Although his choice of weapon (five smooth stones) seemed to be ridiculous, it was a weapon that he had tested. I believe he chose those stones for another reason as well. Although, he knew what he could do with the stones, David also knew what his God had done for him before with even less, and he trusted that if God did it then, He would be with him in this battle as well. The scripture reads,

> "And David said unto Saul, Thy servant was keeping his father's sheep, and when there came a lion, or a bear, and took a lamb out of the flock, I went out after him, and smote him, and delivered it out of his mouth, and when he arose against me, I caught him by his beard, and smote him, and slew him. Thy servant smote both the lion and the bear, and the uncircumcised Philistine shall be as one of them seeing he hath defied the armies of the living God. And David said, Jehovah that delivered me out of the paw of the lion, and out of the paw of the bear, he will deliver me out of the hand of this Philistine." 1 Samuel 17:34–37.

As Christians, our arsenal of weapons is housed in our relationship with God and the Word of God. An arsenal of weapons that is living and active and has been tested and tried for thousands of years without fail. The scripture reads, "For the word of God is living, and active, and sharper than any two-edged sword, and piercing even to the dividing of soul and spirit, of both joints and marrow, and quick to discern the thoughts and intents of the heart." Hebrews 4:12. Accepting Jesus as our Lord and Savior and believing that He died in our place, gives us direct access to the Father in His name. In addition, our acceptance of the finished work of the Lord Jesus gives us the right to claim the promise made by Jesus that whatsoever we ask believing, we shall receive it. The scripture reads, "Whatsoever ye shall ask in my name, that will I do, that the Father may be glorified in the Son." John 14:15–18 This promise goes on to include another Comforter that will abide with us forever. The scripture reads, "But the Comforter, even the Holy Spirit, whom the Father will send in my name, he shall teach you all things, and bring to your remembrance all that I said unto you." John 14:26. Each of us who belong to God through the shed blood of the Lord Jesus Christ has been given a seat in heavenly places with Jesus, and we have been sealed by the Holy Spirit. The same Holy Spirit that Jesus promised to pray to the Father to send into the earth to guide, teach, and comfort the ones who believed on Him. Because of our belief in the Son, we have been made children of God and, we have been given the same authority over all the power of the enemy in the name of Jesus. Jesus told us that we could do the same works that He did and even greater works. The scripture reads, "Verily, verily, I say unto you, he that believeth on me, the works that I do shall he do also, and greater works than these shall he do, because I go unto the Father." John 14:12

As we know, Jesus walked in total authority over the enemy in every area. He not only told us that we could do the exact same things that He did, He also demonstrated this authority for us by the healing of the sick, the raising of the dead, the casting out of demons while here in the earth in a flesh body. He also demonstrated to us how He would always retreat to a place alone to pray and to be alone with the Father before performing any miracles. This time alone with the Father would in some cases last for several hours or for an entire night. He passed this example of how to walk and operate in that authority on to all of us who believe. As this was demonstrated in the lives and activities of the disciples, it must be demonstrated in ours as well as His followers today. The scripture reads, "Behold, I give unto you power to tread on serpents and scorpions, and over all the power of the enemy and nothing shall by any means hurt you." Luke 10:19

We don't have to give up when we go through various attacks of the enemy, we can boldly go before the throne of God in the name of Jesus in faith believing. Even if God does not answer in the exact way we might desire, we still trust Him and will continue to petition Him because we know that He can. This is the kind of faith and belief that Daniel's friends, Shadrach, Meshach, and Abed-nego exhibited when they were faced with being thrown into the fiery furnace. The scripture reads, "If it be so, our God whom we serve is able to deliver us from the burning fiery furnace, and he will deliver us out of thine hand, O king. But if not, be it known unto thee, O king, that we will not serve thy gods, nor worship the golden image which thou hast set up." Daniel 3:17. They had faith in God and stood on their beliefs while speaking what they believed into the atmosphere. Shadrach, Meshach, and Abed-nego stood strong without having the knowledge of Jesus and the Holy Spirit as we do today. We have on-going access to all the power and all the authority of heaven not only with us but within us. As a result, we should be commanding the evil forces in the earth. We should be in control in the earth. We should be in authority in the earth as God has revealed to us in the book of Acts through Paul. He showed us as born again Christians, we are always in charge whatever the particular circumstance. And, it is left up to us to accept our authority and walk in the required faith and belief. The Bible teaches us that Paul was a prisoner on board of a ship sailing to Rome as they encountered a very treacherous storm. Because Paul belonged to God, there was an angel sent to him to reassure him that neither he nor any of the other passengers on board would be hurt in any way. The scripture reads,

> "And now I exhort you to be of good cheer: for there shall be no loss of any man's life among you, but of the ship. For there stood by me this night the angel of God, whose I am, and whom I serve, Saying, Fear not, Paul; thou must be brought before Caesar: and lo, God hath given thee all

them that sail with thee. Wherefore, sirs, be of
good cheer: for I believe God, that it shall be even
as it was told me." Acts 27:22-25.

Because Paul belonged to the God and knew who he was in the
Lord Jesus Christ, he was saved including all that was sailing
with him. As a result of his taking charge and staying in faith, he
believed the angel and took he rightful place of authority in Christ
Jesus. As we know, God is no respecter of persons. Being that Jesus
has already done everything that's needed to be done in order for
us to obey His command to do the same works that He did and
do even greater works, we too can stand and take charge. Because
Jesus went to the Father, we have been given the authority to
command the forces. He told us when He had gone to the Father,
the Holy Spirit would come; whereby, we would be able to keep
His commandments. He kept His word and the Holy Spirit did,
indeed, come to guide and lead us and always takes of Jesus' and
show it unto us. We must not fail our mission, and our mandate to
stand in the gap for the body of Christ and participate in bringing
souls into the kingdom of God. Because of the Holy Spirit, we have
been endowed with the boldness to stand and take our rightful
place of authority in the earth and command the forces. We are to
pray and command from the position of authority instead of from
the position of beggar. Because we're filled with the Holy Spirit,
we will invoke the very same reaction from the demonic forces as
did Jesus. We must command the forces to bow at the name that
is above every name which is the name of Jesus! Remember, the
Lord has not given us a spirit of fear; but of power, and of love and
of a sound mind! Just as David ran to confront Goliath wielding
a slingshot and a stone, we, the Holy Ghost filled saint should run
toward the enemy wielding the power and authority of Almighty
God in the name of Jesus Christ! Now that we know who we are
and what we possess, let's begin commanding the forces!

Conclusion

Prayer of Thanksgiving

Father, thank you for sending your only begotten Son to die in our place. Lord Jesus, thank you for being obedient until death. Thank you Lord Jesus for dying in our place by going to the cross in our stead being crucified, dead, and buried. Thank you for coming out of the grave on the third day as the first begotten of the dead. Thank you for washing us from our sins in your own blood. Thank you for being the first and the last, for having the keys of hell and of death as you promised with all power and authority over all the power of the enemy. Thank you for conquering death and the grave. Thank you for praying the Father to send the Holy Spirit to guide us, to lead us, to take of yours and show it unto us. In Jesus name I pray. Amen.

Statement of Declarations

Where there is the Father, Son, and Holy Ghost,
we have all power and authority! Where there is all
power and authority in Jesus' name, there is strength!
Where there is strength, there is victory!

Prayer for Removal of Spirit of Offense

Father, I choose to always walk in forgiveness to not take up any offense. I am asking you to please forgive me for any unforgiveness and to please remove any offense that has set up in my heart. Thank you for removing unforgiveness and for taking the spirit of offense out of me. Lord, please replace all of it with perfect love. In Jesus' name I pray. Amen.

Intercessory Prayer of Authority

Father, I take authority over all the power of the enemy in Jesus' name. I command every enemy that rise up against us to be destroyed before our face. For it is written, "Every enemy that rise up against us shall be destroyed before our face."

Printed in the United States
By Bookmasters